A COMPLETE HISTORY OF THE
MAFIA

A COMPLETE HISTORY OF THE
MAFIA

JO DURDEN SMITH

METRO BOOKS
NEW YORK

METRO BOOKS
New York

An Imprint of Sterling Publishing
387 Park Avenue South
New York, NY 10016

ISBN: 978-0-7607-9195-0

For information about custom editions, special sales, and premium and corporate purchases, please contact Sterling Special Sales at 800-805-5489 or specialsales@sterlingpublishing.com.

Manufactured in China

5 7 9 10 8 6

www.sterlingpublishing.com

CONTENTS

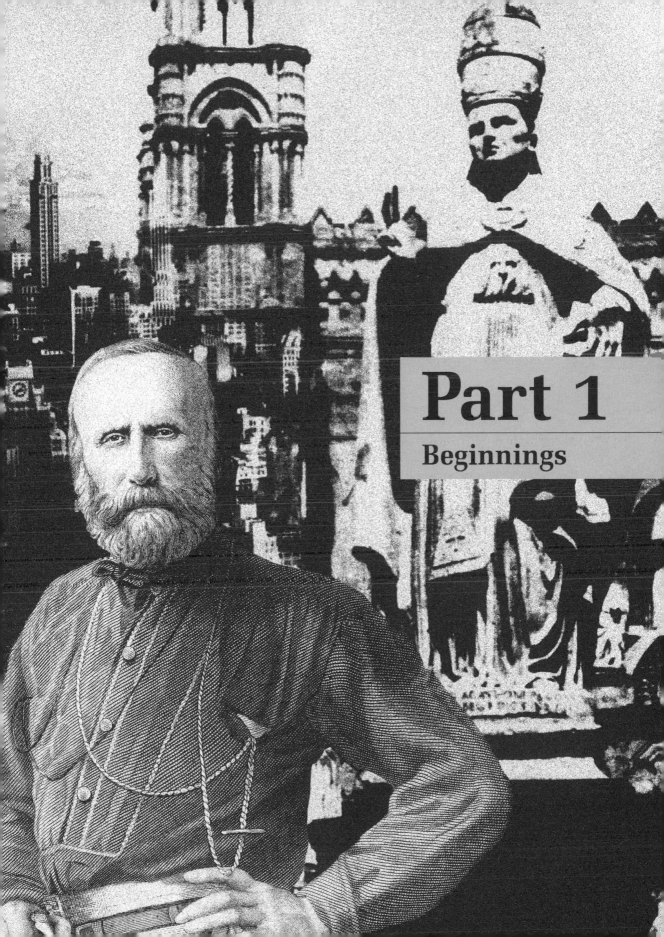

Part 1

Beginnings

1

The Death of Don Calogero Vizzini

W HEN IN THE EARLY 1950s one of the most powerful Mafia bosses in Sicily, Don Calogero Vizzini (known as Don Calò) died, his body was laid in state in a church in his home town of Villalba, where he had been mayor. Politicians from his party, the Christian Democrats, and high Roman Catholic churchmen came to pay their respects, along with the heads of other Mafia families, newspapermen and large numbers of people from the surrounding countryside. On the church door, according to the writer Norman Lewis, was a notice of his death, which read in part: 'Wise, dynamic, tireless, he was the benefactor of the workers on the land and in the sulphur mines. Constantly doing good, his reputation was widespread both in Italy and abroad.

'Great in the face of persecution, greater still in adversity. . . he receives from friends and foes alike the grandest of all tributes: he was a gentleman.'

The notice was not wrong. Though the illiterate ex-farmer, who rarely wore anything more elaborate than baggy trousers and a grimy shirt and could hardly speak anything but his native dialect, may

Il Duce—Italian dictator Mussolini

Sicilian Mafia boss
Don Calogero
Vizzini, a.k.a.
Don Calò

not have been a gentleman in any familiar sense of the word, he had certainly had his share of 'persecution' and 'adversity'. He had spent twenty years in Mussolini's Italy either in jail or on the run from Il Duce's emissary to Sicily, the 'Iron Prefect', Cesare Mori, and he did indeed have 'a reputation' that was 'widespread both in Italy and abroad'. More than anyone else, the slovenly Don Calò had been responsible for the fact that the American part of the invasion of Sicily had been successfully accomplished in a matter of days. Picked up by a special force, and made an honorary colonel in the US Army more or less on the spot, this down-at-heel mayor had ridden with the American spearhead and had become affectionately known as 'General Mafia'.

After the War, Don Calò became a power in the land for the Christian Democrats and at the time of his death he was both rich and immensely powerful. It was therefore not surprising that his flower-decked bier should have been attended by a guard of honour, one of them his successor, Giuseppe Genco Russo. Few people noticed at the time, though, that a cord ran between Russo and his ex-chief's body, a cord down which flowed, by an article of Mafia faith, the ichor or essence of Don Calò's power, preserved into the next generation. If nothing else, the cord signalled the presence of something in the church much older than Christianity, almost as old as the mountainous landscape of Sicily itself.

The Leopard

Some six years later, a book was published which was to become Italy's first-ever international best-seller. It was called *The Leopard*, and the writer was a Sicilian grandee: Giuseppe Tomasi, Prince of Lampedusa and Duke of Palma. It was centred on

Claudia Cardinale
starred as the
beautiful Angelica
Sedàra

Burt Lancaster
played the role of
Don Fabrizio

the figure of the prince's great-grandfather—here called Don Fabrizio—and set at the time of another 'liberation': Garibaldi's arrival in Sicily in the early 1860s prior to the unification of Italy.

The plot of *The Leopard*, inasmuch as there is one, revolves around the prince's nephew, Tancredi, an ardent Garibaldist, who falls in love with a beautiful seventeen-year-old, Angelica Sedàra, whose father is mayor of the area surrounding the prince's summer palace. The mayor is another Don Calogero. He is slovenly, immensely rich and powerful and 'is understood to have been very busy at the time of the liberation'. It is implicit that he is a Mafioso—his 'greedy' and 'overbearing' father-in-law was found dead, with twelve shotgun wounds in his back, two years after Don Calogero's marriage. But he also has, the prince finds out, very great influence in politics: he has rigged the local vote on the question of unification on behalf of his party, so that the result in the area is a unanimous 'yes'. Don Fabrizio, then, when he is invited to become a senator in a new all-Italian parliament, sees the face of the future and recommends Don Calogero Sedàra instead. The Mafia is on its way into politics at a national level as the book moves on.

The Leopard was made into a film by the aristocratic Italian director Luchino Visconti, with Burt Lancaster playing Don Fabrizio, and Alain Delon and Claudia Cardinale, Tancredi and Angelica. It was set firmly in the nineteenth century. But is the book it was based on—in part, at any rate—a portrait of the period immediately after the Second World War? And is Don Calogero Sedàra really Don Calò Vizzini? It is impossible to know. But the picture of the poverty and buried violence in the landscape that is portrayed in the book could be applied to virtually any time in the three or four hundred years before the beginning of the 1960s. Only the clothes, the carriages and the constant presence of the *lupara*, the wolf-shooting shotgun, indeed, prevent it from applying to any time in the past two thousand years.

A countryside well served, for example, 'as a swimming pool, drinking trough, prison, cemetery. It. . . concealed the carcases of beasts and animals until they were reduced to smooth anonymous skeletons.' Village women are seen 'by the flicker of oil lamps. . .[examining] their children's trachoma-inflamed eyelids. They were all of them dressed in mourning and quite a few had been the wives of those scarecrow corpses one stumbles over at the bends in the country tracks.' The poverty in the book is absolute; the riches of the Prince, expressed mostly in vast estates and decaying palaces, are guarded and run by men whose shotguns were 'not

Italian director
Luchino Visconti

always innocuous'. The poverty and the violence in the book, the land, palaces, guards and politics—these could have come from virtually any time. And it was they who provided the mixture peculiar to the island that gave rise to the poisonous historical residue that is the Sicilian Mafia.

2

Sicily: Heartland of the Mafia

S ICILY IS NOT AN ORDINARY ISLAND. For two thousand years before the discovery of America, it paid a very steep price for being at the heart of the Mediterranean Sea, and therefore, roughly speaking, at the strategic centre of the known world. It was a prize to be captured and held, and so it was—by the Greeks, the Romans, the Byzantines, the Arabs, the Germans, the French and any freebooters and *arrivistes* trying to make a name for themselves inbetween. As for its social system, it was the Romans who set the pattern. They systematically deforested Sicily and turned it into a feudal colony whose job was to feed the mainland—and themselves—with wheat. Vast estates worked by slaves stretched all the way across the island; and though the wheat largely disappeared, the estates and the slavery didn't. Long after the world's attention had strayed elsewhere, Sicily remained feudal—peasants were only given the right to own land in the early nineteenth century. Vested interests and the legal chicanery of landlords ensured that very few of them got it until another century or more had passed.

Sicily was in a sense, then, had always been, an island version of Russia, softened by citrus groves planted by the Arabs, but a Russia nonetheless. Three quarters of the island until the beginning of the twentieth century belonged to aristocratic land-lords who shut themselves up in distant palaces or disported themselves in the western European equivalents of Moscow and St. Petersburg. There was no Renaissance or Reformation here, no Enlightenment, no merchants' guilds, city-republics or law-making princes—simply back-breaking toil, a festering resentment of the state, in whatever form it took, and, of course, crime.

From as early as the eighteenth century, banditry and racketeering have always been a recognizable ingredient of Sicilian rural life

Crime in Sicily

Crime in Sicily has always been identified one way and another with island patriotism, with resistance to the occupier. Writers in the eighteenth century described a secret sign language in Sicily which they said dated back to the time of the Greek tyrants. It was also made possible by the sheer difficulty involved in travel into the interior over difficult mountainous terrain. Roads, until the twentieth century, were almost non-existent. Officers of the law were meagre in number and dispersed, and so banditry was for a long time a sound career option for young men, who remained protected from the law if it arrived by clan and family loyalties. These loyalties, particularly those of close kin, overrode everything else. Not for nothing is the basic unit of the Mafia called 'the family'.

In a sense, however, crime was also built into the ancient feudal system. The absentee aristocracy needed managers for their estates, both to ensure and enforce the work of sharecropping peasants, and to protect the land, its buildings and its livestock not only from bandits, but also from the spread of liberal ideas. They needed strong-arm men with local power and influence, men capable of wielding the *lupara* and with not too much respect for the law. The distinction between bandit, 'family'-man and estate security, in other words, was often in the end slight. The managers and the men they hired exacted a price from both sides of the divide for imposing order: a percentage from the peasants for looking after their interests, and a percentage from the masters for continuing to insure theirs. Meanwhile of course they could themselves freelance as the very bandits they were supposed to be providing security against. The protection racket was from very early times a particular Sicilian speciality. There was immense pressure on landlords to hire bands of brigands as their personal *guardani*, and co-operation with the forces of law was virtually unknown.

One reason for the lack of co-operation was that though the state was totalitarian, the laws which upheld it in Sicily were a mess of conflicting statutes produced by successive invaders. Court cases were interminable and it was in everyone's interests—the peasants, the outlaws, the aristocracy and the officers of the court—that the law's delay should be short. Many judges, after all, had to buy their posts; clerks of the court were paid little or nothing. It was therefore expected that a 'man of influence' would soon come calling or else would take care of the matter himself. One eighteenth century traveller recorded the existence in Sicily of a secret justice society more effective than the courts, one in which all members were sworn to obey its judgments.

Banditry, the protection racket, anti-liberal politics, bribery, secret justice societies, families: everything that created the Sicilian Mafia, then, was already in place well before the nineteenth century—everything, that is, except perhaps its name.

3

The Mafia Emerges

THE WORD 'MAFIA', according to the historian Denis Mack Smith, first appeared officially in Sicily in 1863, when a dialect play based on life in the city's main prison opened in Palermo. It was called *I Mafiosi della Vicaria*, and it popularised a word already used by criminals and by landlords looking for strong-arms. What its origins are is still unclear. There have been suggestions that it derives from the Arabic *ma fia* or 'place of refuge', used by the Arabs after the Norman invasion when they were enslaved on their new conquerors' estates. Others have suggested it comes from a secret acronym used by Sicilians when they rose up against the Normans, or from *mahjas*, the Arabic word for boasting. But whatever the word's origins, the people now identified by it had been at work long before it became common usage.

The names of gangs were first recorded in the eighteenth century, the Beati Paoli, the Revengers, and so are the names of an individual bandit or two, like Don Sferlazza, a seminarist and outlaw involved in a family vendetta who as a priest was immune

from punishment. Kidnappings for ransom were frequent, according to the records, as were cattle-rustling, food-smuggling and illegal control of water-sources. There was even a popular religious cult of the criminal called the Decollati, in which prayers were offered to executed criminals in shrines full of dismembered bones.

But the gangs only came out into the open collectively with the rebellion of 1848 against the island's Bourbon rulers, when they swept into Palermo from the countryside to join in. Battle was joined with one gang led by a ferocious woman goatherd called Testa Di Lana, who had a vendetta against the police. By the time order was restored, the Sicilian state had virtually collapsed, and gangs like the Little Shepherds and the Cut-throats were, according to Mack Smith, 'the one flourishing form of association in Sicily. The chief of police had to co-operate with some of them, so Scordato, the illiterate peasant boss of Bagheria, and Di Miceli of Monreale, were now employed as tax collectors and coastguards and became rich. Law enforcement at Misilmeri was handed over to the famous bandit Chinnici, who found a common denominator between lucrative kidnapping and the suppression of liberalism.'

Beyond the Unification of Italy

Liberalism, though it was the enemy of their aristocratic sponsors, was in the end, however, to be the friend of the Mafiosi. When Garibaldi arrived to

Palermo, Sicily—
the city that saw
the birth of the
word 'Mafia'

Entered according to act of Congress A.D. 1869 by Johnson, Fry & Co. in the clerks office of the district court for the Southern district of New York.

G. Garibaldi

start the unification of Italy, he found the gangs useful, if unreliable, allies. And when unification finally arrived, the Mafiosi—as they were later to do in Russia—found it all too easy to subvert the liberal institutions he instituted. The first national election gave them a new tool: the manipulation and delivery of votes. Trial by jury virtually guaranteed them impunity, since few individuals were brave enough or rich enough to want to stand up to them publicly with a verdict of 'guilty'. Charities and credit institutions became grist to their mill, and even the new Bank of Sicily was not immune. They used it to channel funds to their political allies. An early director of the Bank was first kidnapped and then murdered after irregularities were found.

Neither liberalism nor unification, though, did anything at all to improve the ordinary peasant's lot. Nor did it do anything for Sicily as a going economic concern. Taxes went up and so did food prices. The local silk and textile industries collapsed. Hostility against the mainland, the national government and its institutions everywhere grew— amongst churchmen, aristocrats, lawyers, peasants. Everyone, whenever necessary, now used the good offices of the Mafia, even though its stocks-in-trade were violence and fear. In the 1860s, the British consul in Palermo wrote:

'Secret societies are all-powerful. *Camorre* and *maffie* [sic], self-elected juntas, share the earnings of the workmen, keep up intercourse with outcasts and take malefactors under their wing and protection.'

A decade later, an Italian government report stated bluntly:

'Violence is the only prosperous industry in Sicily.'

Garibaldi recognized the influence of Italy's gangs in his quest to unify the country

Every Sicilian for Sicily and the Mafia

The degree to which even the Church and the landowning aristocrats grew into collusion with the Mafia at such an early date seems now extraordinary. Palaces were opened up to assassins, and the local Catholic Church hierarchy—which regarded the north and its government as godless—at best turned a very blind eye. At worst, in the words of a report written by a northern MP in the 1870s: 'There is a story about a former priest who became the crime leader in a town near Palermo and administered the last rites to some of his own victims. After a certain number of these stories the perfume of orange and lemon blossoms starts to smell of corpses.'

Seventy years later, the Mafia bandit Salvatore Giuliano used to attend tea-parties at the Archbishop's Palace in Palermo, even though he was at the time a prisoner in Ucciardone prison. Another Archbishop, forty years on, declared that Tommaso Buscetta, the first and most important of the witnesses finally to give evidence against the Mafia, was one of the three greatest enemies of Sicily. This was just two years after the word 'Mafia' had entered the Italian criminal code for the very first time, even though it had been denounced as relying on official protection by an Italian Minister of Justice over a hundred years before. The response at that time was to become a litany from then on, both in Sicily and later in America: 'The Mafia is a fabrication: the invention of northern policemen. . .'

4

The Mafia Moves to America: First Stop, New Orleans

IN 1880, NEAR THE RAILROAD STATION at Lecrera, Sicily, an English clergyman was kidnapped by a bandit leader called Leoni and held for a ransom of £5000. While the authorities dithered, one of his ears was cut off and sent to them in a parcel—at which point the British began to pay attention. The negotiations, though, took time, and Leoni, growing impatient, cut off the other ear and delivered it with a note saying that the clergyman would be history unless the ransom money arrived very soon. The British duly paid up and recovered their hapless—and by now earless—national. But so strong was their protest to the Italian government that it was forced to send an army after Leoni. Leoni and most of his followers were subsequently killed in a battle. But one of them, Giuseppe Esposito, escaped and made his way to America, to New Orleans, where there was a substantial Italian community, and where he is said to have bought a fishing boat, named it *Leoni* and had the bandit's flag flown at its mast.

Esposito, though, also began shaking down the prosperous shopkeepers and restaurateurs in New

Orleans' Italian community, forcing them to invest in a fleet of small boats. He organized a gang of his own, in imitation of Leoni's, called the 'Black Hand'. In the process, though, he ran foul of another Italian, who seems also to have been in the protection business, one Tony Labruzzo. Labruzzo shopped Esposito to the Italian consul and the New Orleans police chief put two of his best men, brothers David and Mike Hennessy, on the case. They soon arrested Esposito, who was rapidly deported back to Palermo, where he was sentenced to life imprisonment.

Esposito's Legacy: The Black Hand

There were, however, repercussions. Tony Labruzzo was assassinated long before Esposito came to trial and it wasn't long before two more brothers, saloon-keepers Charles and Tony Matranga, took over the Black Hand. They started out with the usual kind of racket: the provision of dock-hands, under duress, to Joe and Pete Provenzano, grocery-store owners who had a monopoly on the unloading of fruit-ships from South America. Then they decided simply to take over the monopoly, and they even started going after the Provenzanos' grocery stores. Suddenly there were armed men, from both sides, in the streets. Two men on the Provenzano side were killed and many wounded in an ambush.

The police chief in New Orleans by this time was David Hennessy, one of the two brothers who'd arrested and deported Giuseppe Esposito some years before. He liked the Provenzanos and he was anxious to see their attackers brought to book as quickly as possible. So he corresponded with the central headquarters of the *carabinieri* in Rome, asking for the names and photographs of Leoni's old gang. He was warned off by an anonymous letter, but he persisted. In October 1890 he was assassinated.

Feelings in New Orleans ran high as eleven Italians listed in Hennessy's files were rapidly arrested and they remained high as another ten were added to those behind bars. Seven of the accused were tried together on the charge of Hennessy's murder in February 1891. But it was clear soon enough that both the judge and jury had been tampered with. Though there were witnesses to the crime, and though one of the defendants had actually confessed to attending a Mafia meeting at which Hennessy's death had been decreed, the judge released two of the accused in the early stages, and the jury did the same for the rest. There were celebrations in the Italian community that night. A group of Sicilians trampled the Stars and Stripes in the mud and then hung it upside down beneath the Italian flag.

Advertisements were quickly placed in the newspapers of March 14 summoning 'all good citizens' to a mass meeting, 'prepared for action'. A mob gathered. One of the sponsors of the meeting handed out guns and eleven of the twelve men still behind bars were promptly lynched.

From this point, the Mafia in New Orleans went quite quiet. But there was another flare-up in 1907, when a seven-year-old Italian was kidnapped for a $6000 ransom and then killed. Four of the gang were quickly caught, and one of them was hanged. But it became clear during the course of the proceedings that businesses in the Italian community had been paying protection money to Sicilian gangs for years.

5

The Mafia in New York

NEARLY ONE AND A QUARTER million immigrants left southern Italy for the United States between 1900 and 1910, a high proportion of them from Sicily, driven out by poverty and the relentless grind of semi-slavery, the oppression of landlords and high taxes. Many of them made their first landing in New York; and it is New York's police records that provide another glimpse of Sicilian gangs operating behind the camouflage of their own communities, and at the same time preying on them.

Most often, one must assume, New York's police force paid little attention to crime in the teeming Italian sections of the city. But murder was another matter, especially such a series of murders as occurred in 1902 and 1903. The male victims were found in barrels, crates or sacks and in many cases their tongues had been slit in two. They were clearly talkers who'd broken the law of omertà— manly silence. A Sicilian gang boss called Giuseppe Morello was immediately suspected. He was running a counterfeit ring, sending his product all over the United States, and the police were already on his track, together with that of his chief lieutenants, known to them as Lupo 'the Wolf' and Petto 'the Ox'.

In April 1903 they began to make real progress. On April 13 another body was found with its head almost severed, this time in a barrel near a pile of lumber on the Lower East Side. The victim wore earrings, which strongly suggested that he was Sicilian. His photograph was soon recognised by a detective as a man he'd recently seen keeping company with the Wolf and the Ox at a restaurant owned by Sicilian Pietro Inzerillo. The barrel came from a wholesale grocer who'd supplied it to Inzerillo's restaurant.

The case was handed over at this point to an Italian detective called Joseph Petrosino, who went to visit a member of Morello's gang who was behind bars in Sing Sing prison. The convict, Joseph de Priemo, immediately recognised the photograph of the dead man Petrosino showed him. It was his brother-in-law Beneditto Maradonia, a fact later confirmed by Maradonia's wife.

It seemed like an open-and-shut case. In Morello's house the police found a letter from Maradonia, saying that he could no longer remain in the dangerous business of distributing fake money and was going to go back to his family in Buffalo. Morello, Inzerillo, the Wolf, the Ox and several others were arrested. De Priemo and members of Maradonia's family, however, refused to repeat the evidence they'd given to the police in court and the men had to be freed. Morello and the Wolf were later charged with counterfeiting and sent down on thin evidence for twenty-five and thirty years respectively. Inzerillo, too, was given a draconian sentence on the charge of 'altering his citizenship papers'.

Links between America and Sicily

The Ox, still at large, retired to Browntown, Pennsylvania, where he was shot down in 1925 shortly after De Priemo was released from Sing Sing. Inzerillo was also assassinated soon after he was released from prison. As for the detective Joseph Petrosino, he remained intensely curious about the Sicilian Mafia and in 1908, with special permission from his boss, police chief Joseph Bingham, he set off for Palermo to ask some questions.

He travelled, under conditions of intense secrecy, as Guglielmo De Simone, with an address at the Banco Commerciale in Palermo. But someone talked—and there is said to have been a meeting of the Black Hand in New Orleans which sent word forward that he was coming to one of the most powerful chieftains in Sicily, Don Vito Cascio Ferro.

Don Vito is believed today to have been as close as anyone to unifying the often-warring gangs of Sicilian Mafiosi and creating a syndicate. He streamlined extortion and kidnapping and sent emissaries to America as ambassadors. He had boats for smuggling cattle and food, as well as powerful political friends. So it was Don Vito personally who shot down Petrosino as he walked across Marina Square in Palermo on March 12, 1909. He boasted publicly about it. It was a matter of honour and a demonstration to all who took notice of Don Vito's untouchability.

By the time of Don Vito's ascendancy to what may have been the *capo di tutti capi* of Sicily, many immigrants were beginning to filter back to the island from the United States, bringing with them news of democracy and of the easy pickings to be had. The idea of long-distance co-operation across

Overleaf: New York's Times Square: the city greeted 1,250,000 Italian immigrants between 1900 and 1910

the Atlantic must have grown. The First World War, though, was soon to put the idea on hold. Though Mafiosi in Sicily like Don Calogero Vizzini are said to have made a fortune from war shortages, crime rates in the United States fell drastically as its young men went off to fight.

After the War, too, there were further delays. A quota system was introduced in the United States which stemmed immigration from Sicily. But the island had problems of its own. In 1924, Mussolini's prefect, Cesare Mori, took over, and like Mussolini himself, Mori had not the slightest interest in due process. He strung Mafia leaders up from lamp-posts. He besieged whole towns where their presence was suspected. In the little town of Gangi, he arrested, captured and convicted 100 Mafiosi, including a woman, the so-called Queen of Gangi, who dressed like a man. He put behind bars leaders like Don Ciccio Cuccia and Don Calogero Vizzini; and though some were released for lack of evidence, the Mafia took the severest beating in its entire history. Murders on the island declined by three-quarters, and the population was struck dumb. When Mori offered a prize for the best essay on how to destroy the Mafia, not a single entry was received.

It took, in fact, the arrival of the Second World War and the toppling of Mussolini for the idea to be revived—as it was, with a considerable vengeance. In the interim the baton of crime was passed to America, where the Sicilian Mafia was to grow exponentially through the unique growth medium of Prohibition.

The Mafia Oath and the Appearance of Cosa Nostra

When Don Tommaso Buscetta in 1984 began to

speak about the inner workings of the Mafia to Palermo magistrate Giovanni Falcone, the word Mafia had only recently been added to the Italian criminal code, and editions of the *Oxford English Dictionary* still extant, according to the writer Peter Robb in his remarkable book *Midnight in Sicily*, said of the word 'Mafia': 'often erroneously supposed to constitute an organized secret society existing for criminal purposes.'

Buscetta forced a change in the Dictionary's definition. He exposed everything to Falcone: the chains of command, the intergang wars, the deep connections between America and Sicily. He also described the oath that had to be taken by every Mafia recruit. It is worth quoting in full, for it has odd pre-Christian echoes of the cord which passed between the body of Don Calogero Vizzini and his successor. It also gives the real name of the Mafia for the very first time. Buscetta said:

'The neophyte is brought to a secluded spot, which could even be someone's home, in the presence of three or more Men of Honour of the family. Then the oldest of those present informs him that the purpose of *questa cosa*—this thing—is to protect the weak and to eliminate the oppressors. Then a finger is pricked on one of the hands of the person being sworn in and the blood is made to fall on a sacred image. Then the image is placed in his hand and is burned. At this time the neophyte must endure the fire, passing the sacred image quickly from one hand to the other until it goes out, and he swears to remain faithful to the principles of the Cosa Nostra (Our Thing), stating solemnly: 'May my flesh burn like this holy picture if I am unfaithful to this oath.'

'This in broad outline was the method of swearing in use when I became a member of the Cosa Nostra. After the swearing-in, and only then, the

Man of Honour is introduced to the head of the family, whose post he did not know about before-hand, knowing even less about the existence of the Cosa Nostra *per se.*'

Until that moment in 1984, the real name of the Mafia that had grown within the Sicilian state had never been known to any outsider. Neither it, nor the existence of the Cosa Nostra in America, could any longer be denied.

Part 2
Expansion

6
Prohibition

President Calvin Coolidge brought in Prohibition, and opened up new avenues for organized crime

Coolidge's Volstead Act turned the United States into a 'dry' nation

PRESIDENT CALVIN COOLIDGE called the Volstead Act, which brought in Prohibition on January 17, 1920, 'the greatest social experiment of modern times'. But what it was, in fact, was the last stand of rock-ribbed White Anglo-Saxon America against the tide of beer- and wine-drinking immigrants it imagined to be polluting the clean, clear water of the state. It had been presented as a patriotic issue by those who had ruthlessly campaigned for it during the First World War—and now they were victorious. Germans drank beer, they'd said; we are at war against Germany. Thus, to be consistently patriotic, we must also wage war against beer. The same soon went for the Italians and their wine, for the dirt farmers avoiding taxes on spirits with their illegal stills, and it certainly went for the saloons across the country where the lower sort of worker drank away the pain of underpayment, unemployment and appalling conditions, both at work and at home. Besides, the keepers of saloons were notorious as organizers of the local vote for any politician with the ability to pay for them. They were major

The authorities were hard pressed to stem the tide of illegal liquor during prohibition

polluters of the Founding Fathers' body politic—and they had to go too.

It was clear, from the very beginning, that it was an act of monumental moral and political stupidity. Not only did the Act have a number of loopholes—such as the production and prescription of 'medicinal' and 'agricultural' alcohol and of wine

used for religious purposes—it was never backed by ordinary citizens. And it was they, who, by exercising what they saw as their God-given right to go on drinking, handed power to the rum-runners and speakeasy-operators and those who controlled them. They voted them, in effect, into office as a sort of underground government. Not for nothing was Al Capone in Cicero, Illinois nicknamed 'The Mayor of Crook County'.

The process by which Americans gradually—and fatally—lost their capacity for moral indignation began virtually immediately. Within an hour of Prohibition's arrival, six armed men in Chicago made off with $100,000-worth of whisky that had been earmarked for medicinal use. Within a matter of weeks, 15,000 doctors and 57,000 retail druggists had applied for licences to sell this same kind of hooch for any ache and pain they could find. In 1917, before any of the states had voted to turn themselves dry—as many did one by one—Americans had consumed two billion gallons of hard liquor, and everyone who had any kind of capacity to do so was suddenly racing to make sure that they went right on drinking them. One of the biggest of the early bootleggers, a Chicago lawyer and pharmacist called George Remus, who moved to Cincinnati to set up his business, was soon bringing in $20 million a year. It would have been $40 million, but the other $20 million had to go to bent cops and Prohibition agents, to biddable judges and politicians.

The Corruption of Politics: Warren Harding

Did Warren Harding oversee the most corrupt administration in America's history?

The White House became a popular locale for Harding's cronies

Remus and others like him were enormously helped by the fact that the White House was by now occupied by perhaps the most corrupt administration in America's history: that of Warren Harding. Harding was a blow-hard, womanizing nobody from Marion, Ohio, who'd always been a useful tool for corrupt party politicians in his home state. He'd become a senator in 1915, and then the last-minute compromise candidate for president at the Republican convention in 1919. He campaigned mostly from his own front porch in Marion, projecting a dream of the past: of an America of small towns and simple values, God-fearing and centred on the family.

When he arrived at the White House, he brought

with him a family of his own, his campaign managers and poker-playing cronies, who promptly turned the business of government into a machine for lining their own pockets. His Attorney General, Harry Daugherty, for example, was always on hand to block investigations and organize pardons— open, in fact, to any scam at all through his bagman Jess Smith. They gathered over the booze upstairs at the White House with the President. Members of Congress were often found drunk on the floor of the House and the library of the Senate was reckoned to be the best bar in Washington DC.

Remus and the rest were also assisted by the fact that Prohibition agents were not made part of the United States' civil service. Instead, their recruitment was handed over to local politicians and became part of their 'bag', their area of patronage. The agents were also paid a minimum salary, one that was virtually an open invitation to corruption. But both politicians and agents were only part of a long line who were now queuing up for their share in the spoils. Corruption was little by little becoming a quintessential part of local, as well as national government—and nowhere more so than in Chicago.

Chicago under 'Big Bill' Thompson

Overleaf:
Gangs came to prominence in the Windy City during the early twentieth century

Prohibition arrived in Illinois—and thus in Chicago—in 1918, under the mayoralty of 'Big Bill' Thompson. Thompson was the son of a native Bostonian who'd made a fortune in real estate in 'the Windy City'. He never finished high school, and left home at fourteen to become first a brakeman on the Union Pacific Railroad, and then an apprentice cowboy in Cheyenne. His father later bought him a ranch in Nebraska, but after he died, 'Big Bill'

returned to Chicago, became a star sportsman at the Chicago Athletic Club, and decided, on a bet, to run for city alderman on the Republican ticket in 1900.

By 1915, this tub-thumping, foul-talking stentor of a man had been elected Mayor and as Mayor he inherited all the shady connections between politics and crime that past Democratic administrations had spawned. The rackets of the Chicago gangs—prostitution, gambling, slot-machines, labour-racketeering and so on—had always been shared out even-handedly between the inner-city wards, whose bosses provided political protection. In return, at election time, the gangs made sure that as many of the votes as possible—real or not—went the right way. This was an arrangement that suited everyone. Violence was kept to a minimum, and the pickings were good for all—particularly for 'Big Jim' Colosimo, who controlled most of the slot-machines and brothels in the city and had a popular saloon called Diamond Jim's.

Thompson immediately became an enthusiastic participant in this cosy arrangement, and little by little turned Chicago's city government into a miniature version of the Harding administration that was to come. With protection from above—a venal governor of Illinois called Ed Small—he turned City Hall into a personal cash cow. Every permission, every licence, every job now came at a price—even the garbage collectors had to pay $5 a year to his Republican Fund for every horse and cart. Meanwhile he appointed a series of corrupt police chiefs, wound down Chicago's Morals Division, and made sure that the cops regularly took 'advice' from his ward-level political chieftains. He also created in each ward what were called 'honorary precinct captaincies'—one of which was awarded to Colosimo in 1919, the year before he was killed.

Colosimo was killed because he just didn't get it—and his bodyguard Johnny Torrio did. Prohibition had come and Johnny Torrio, a friend of George Remus, just knew that moving heavily into booze would make them more money than anyone could imagine. What's more, he had a relative in town at the time who not only agreed with him, but could also get rid once and for all of Colosimo's opposition: a young hood from New York called Alfonso Capone.

7

Al Capone

NEAPOLITAN IN BACKGROUND, Al Capone was born in 1899 in New York and grew up into a resourceful small-time hood, working in the rackets and as a bouncer in a Brooklyn brothel where a knife-fight gave him his nickname: 'Scarface'. In New York, if he'd stayed there, he might never have amounted to much. But in 1920, when on the run from the police, he got the all-important invitation from Chicago. Nominally, he became Torrio's body-guard—but he was, in effect, his hit-man. Sent by Torrio to make Colosimo's acquaintance at his saloon-headquarters one night, he coolly gunned him down.

From then on, it was a partnership: Torrio and Capone, Capone and Torrio. They took over Colosimo's brothels, and then moved immediately into large-scale bootlegging, under the protection of the Mayor and his police. When, in 1923, Thompson decided not to run again, leaving the way open to a Democratic candidate, they simply upped sticks and moved their operation to the nearby city of Cicero, where the next local elections were conducted, more or less literally, at the point of their hoodlums' guns. Cicero soon became a

Al Capone:
one of the most
recognizable crime
figures in history

Bugs Moran,
O'Bannion's
lieutenant and
bitter rival to
Capone

The aftermath of
the Valentine's Day
Massacre, 1929

modern version of a Wild West frontier-town, full of speakeasies and brothels. It had greyhound racing and what was probably at the time the highest-stakes casino in the world.

With their own turf secure, they were now ready to move back in to claim the main prize, Chicago. This brought them into direct competition with the mainly Irish gang of 'Deanie' O'Bannion, a genial ex-choirboy and journalist who served only the finest liquor and ran his business from the city's most fashionable flower-shop. For a while both sides held their hand. But then in November 1924, in revenge for a trick which got Torrio a police record (and eventually nine months in jail), O'Bannion was killed by three of Torrio's men in his shop, after they'd arrived to order a funeral wreath.

The death of O'Bannion, who was buried in high style, triggered an all-out war for control of the Chicago liquor trade, with Torrio and Capone pitted against O'Bannion's lieutenants and heirs, Hymie Weiss and 'Bugs' Moran, and also against the four brothers of the Sicilian Genna family, who had a licence to make agricultural alcohol. The going soon got too hot for Johnny Torrio, who in 1925 retired to Naples, taking $50 million, it's said, with him. But Capone was made of sterner—and more cunning—stuff. He gradually eliminated the Genna family and as he did so he bought politicians and judges, journalists and police brass, until he was in effect in control, not only of all enforcement agencies and public opinion, but also of City Hall. He made massive donations to the 1927 campaign of Mayor 'Big Bill' Thompson, who'd decided to run again. With his man safely in office, he held court to all comers in fifty rooms on two floors of the downtown Metropole Hotel, where he projected

Chicago saw Capone come to prominence as a crime lord

himself to reporters as an eccentric businessman and philanthropist. He even set up soup kitchens in Chicago at the beginning of the Great Depression.

In 1929, having already got rid of Hymie Weiss, he was finally ready to move against his last surviving enemy, Bugs Moran. Word was passed to Moran that a consignment of hijacked booze could be picked up at a garage on North Clark Street on St. Valentine's Day, but soon after his people arrived, so did Capone's torpedoes, two of them in police uniform. Six of Moran's men died in what became known as the St. Valentine's Massacre, along with an unfortunate optometrist who liked hanging out with hoods. Moran himself only escaped because he was late for the appointment. As for Capone, he was on holiday that day in Biscayne Bay, Florida, and on the phone to the Miami DA at the time of the slaughter at the SMC Cartage Company garage.

In the end Capone was brought to book, not by the cops or the FBI—despite the myth of Elliot Ness and *The Untouchables*—but by the internal revenue service. In 1931, he was tried for tax evasion and sentenced to jail for eleven years. By the time he came out eight years later, the Mafia had moved on, had become more sophisticated. He himself was not only old hat but half mad from tertiary syphilis. He died in his bed eight years later on his Florida estate. Bugs Moran outlived him by ten years.

8
New York

WHAT HAPPENED IN CHICAGO happened in more or less the same way in New York—except that there the pickings were even bigger. New York was not only near the Canadian border, as Chicago was, it was also on the Atlantic Ocean. So the gangs who came to control the liquor trade had New York City's docks at their disposal, as well as the coves and inlets of Long Island. They controlled, in effect, not only the distribution side in America's largest city, but also their product's major points of entry into the United States.

New York was also, of course—and had always been—the single most important point of entry for another important commodity: immigrants. Millions of people, on the run from poverty, bigotry, authoritarianism and famine in Europe, had made their first landfall at Ellis Island, before debarking into the swarming streets and tenements of the city. And once there, they tended naturally to cling together in their own neighbourhoods, with the new arrivals learning the ropes from their own kind. There were, of course, overlaps, as well as

New York was seen as a brave New World and a land of opportunity for many of southern Italy's ambitious young men

inevitable frictions, as they jostled and rubbed shoulders with communities of other nationalities. The gangs that rose up in the districts where each succeeding wave of immigrants settled were both soldiers in inter-community wars and necessary enforcers of peace.

It was, first of all, a matter of real protection. Soldiers were a necessity to protect against invasion—and also, given that the poor will always prey upon the poor, against crime, both from inside and outside. The turf, the territory, had to be defended; businesses within it had to be guaranteed and disputes had to be settled via some system that ensured at least a minimal amount of justice. These, in each of the communities that successively rolled up on America's shore, became the roles of the strongarms, the reckless, who found more than enough promising raw material for their armies in young men hungry for money and advancement in the brave New World.

By the time of the First World War, the early immigrants of the nineteenth century, mostly Irish and German, who'd followed this pattern, had by and large settled in. The Germans had gone into business or migrated westward while the Irish had moved into politics and saloon-keeping—though many had also joined the police, where employment was regular and the opportunties for earning extra money on the side great. But the newer arrivals, among them Italians, Jews and a second wave of poor German immigrants, were still yet to make their mark. It was from them that the gangs—and the Mafia—of the modern period emerged, and the word 'protection' took on its contemporary meaning: that of protection against the 'protectors'.

Protection in this sense, of course, had always been a specialty of the Sicilian Mafia, but it was also

Immigrants became an important commodity for New York's gangs

People were
recruited into gangs
even as they got
their first taste of
America at Ellis
Island

a natural outgrowth of the local gangs' function, whatever their nationality. It was also immeasurably boosted in the new immigrant's home by two further elements they came across largely for the first time: industrialization and the rise of the trade union movement.

Labour Racketeering and 'Little Augie' Orgen

Both before and after the First World War, the fledgeling trade unions in New York set about organizing any industry they could find, from clothing-workers in sweatshops to hauliers to stevedores in the docks—using the only weapon they had against the employers: strikes. The employers responded by hiring scab labour and/or sending in goons to intimidate the strikers. Both

The Mafia of the modern America emerged from those whose first view of the country was the Statue of Liberty

sides, in other words, found themselves in need of solid muscle: the unions to protect their striking workers and to beat off scabs, and the employers to keep out union organizers and to bring the strikers to heel. The gangs, in other words, became necessary warriors on both sides in a struggle that not only crossed community borders, but was also city-wide. And they used this to their considerable advantage.

What they chose to do—particularly a visionary called Jacob 'Little Augie' Orgen—was to play both sides against the middle, to make themselves so necessary to both employers and trade unions that in the end they were able, little by little, to take over percentages—often large percentages—of both. From the period after the First World War stems the Mafia's ongoing and serpentine involvement both in American trade unions and in a huge range of seemingly legitimate businesses which still pay dues to 'the friends'.

This system of two-way protection became known to law-enforcement as labour racketeering, and it had a profound effect on the growth of what came to be the American Cosa Nostra in New York. In opening up the city, it broke down the barriers between immigrant communities, and made possible the co-operation of Jews, Germans and Italians in crime. By the time Prohibition arrived with its huge new opportunities, the seeds of a powerful alliance had been sown, an alliance that was symbolised by the first meeting of two of the most important men in American crime history: Lucky Luciano and Meyer Lansky.

9

The Sicilian and the Jew: Lucky Luciano and Meyer Lansky

Meyer Lansky became one of the most influential members of the Cosa Nostra

MEYER LANSKY, born Maier Suchowjansky in Grodno, Poland, arrived in New York in about 1916, at the age of fourteen. He seems to have taken a job as an engineering apprentice. But he was soon part of the rough-and-tumble of the

Lucky Luciano said
he had 'an instant
kind of understand-
ing' with future
long time confeder-
ate Meyer Lansky

Lower East Side's streets, running with the Jewish gangs and fighting for both territory and survival. It was then, some time around 1917, that he somehow ran across Lucky Luciano.

The story of how they met is variously told: Lansky was defending a prostitute who was being beaten up. He outfaced Luciano in a street-rumble; or they met in a prison cell with Bugsy Siegel. But however they met, Luciano later said of their first encounter: 'We had an instant kind of understanding. It may sound crazy, but if anyone wants to use the expression 'blood brothers', then surely Meyer and I were like that.'

The second member of what was to become the most important partnership in the history of the Mafia was born Salvatore Lucania, and arrived in New York from Sicily with his parents at the age of ten. Almost immediately in trouble with the police for theft and later drug-peddling, he seems, by the time he met Lansky, to have graduated into a torpedo for 'Little Augie' Orgen—though he was almost certainly also a 'made' man inside the family of an old fashioned Sicilian Don called Giuseppe Masseria. Luciano soon co-opted Lansky into 'Little Augie's' gang as a strategist during the early days of Prohibition. But it wasn't long before they decided to move into booze with a man who Lansky is supposed to have met at a *bar mitzvah*, a man who was to take the rough street-edges off them both: the legendary Arnold Rothstein.

Arnold Rothstein

Arnold Rothstein always dressed the part

Arnold Rothstein was one of a kind. If the Mafia has glamour, then it was he who first injected it, dressing in wing-tips, fedoras, top hats, tuxedos and silk suits. If it is associated with fancy casinos, then it was he who opened the first of them in New York City, and brought craps in from the streets to the brushed green baize. If it is synonymous with Prohibition and the running of booze, he was the first big thinker, bringing shipfuls of it from Europe in the very early days. And if it is pleading the Fifth Amendent that comes to mind, then that was all A.R. too: his own lawyer took the right to plead the Fifth all the way to the Supreme Court and saw it turned into law.

The Mafia made a fortune from more glamorous pastimes such as gambling

Rothstein was not a poor boy off the streets like the other early Jewish gangsters, men like Lansky and 'Dutch' Schultz. His father—religious, generous to charities and politically well connected—had a dry goods store, a cotton plant and a house on New York's Upper East Side. But from the age of fifteen Rothstein seems to have been attracted to the roister and turbulence of the downtown neighborhoods: the gambling, the rackets, the booze. He may have meant to go straight, but it was his father in the end who made up his mind for him. When he married a *shiksa*, he was disinherited, declared dead—and that was that.

He made his way at first as a gambler—it remained till his death his greatest love. And it was through gambling that he first became a legend in the underworld when, faced with a ringer, a pool shark specially brought in from Philadelphia to teach him a lesson, he beat him—and all those who'd bet on him—in a forty-hour session, by sheer will.

Doors at this point began to open to him and he soon became a protégé of Big Tim Sullivan, the political boss of the Lower East Side. With Sullivan's help he opened a glamorous midtown casino, and became the key to the door to rich New Yorkers wanting any sort of good time.

With more money from the casino than he could spend on himself—and holding court every night at Lindy's diner on Broadway—Rothstein now entered a new career, as an underworld banker, backing any project that took his fancy: drugs, brothels, fixed fights. If Gatsby in F. Scott Fitzgerald's *The Great Gatsby* is based on Cincinnati boot-legger George Remus, then Rothstein appears as Meyer Wolfhiem, the man who in the novel fixed the 1919 World Series— though in fact Rothstein had refused. He said it was a fine idea, but it would create too much mayhem if it ever came out.

He did, though, agree to back the first major booze-running operation after the passing of the Volstead Act, though only on condition that he was more than an investor: this time he had to be boss. He bought fast speedboats to bring the booze off the ships that he ordered as they waited in international waters; he paid off the police every step of the way to New York; and he employed as soldiers and drivers a great many men who were soon to become kingpins of the city's Mafia: Siegel, Luciano, Lansky, Schultz, Louis Lepke, 'Legs' Diamond, Frank Costello (born Francesco Castiglia) and more.

He did it for the money, but also for the good times—and the good times weren't to last. On Sunday November 24, 1928, he had a phone call at Lindy's asking for a meeting about a gambling debt he owed to a Californian. The game had been rigged in his view, and he'd refused to pay. But he took no gun to the meeting at the Park Central Hotel, since that was against etiquette, and he was later found shot in the stomach in the lobby. He died in the Polyclinic Hospital a few days later, after a visit from his estranged wife.

'Legs' Diamond and associates

10

New York and Prohibition

By 1927 there were over 30,000 speakeasies in New York City alone

PROHIBITION IN NEW YORK was a farce. By 1922 there were at least 5000 speakeasies in the City and by 1927 over 30,000—twice the number of legal bars, restaurants and nightclubs there'd been in New York before Prohibition began. There were thirty-eight on East 52nd Street alone, according to the writer Robert Benchley—and all this was quite apart from fancy nightspots like the Stork Club, opened in 1927 by an Oklahoman bootlegger called Sherman

Columnist Walter
Winchell was one
of the more famous
guests of the Stork
Club

Jimmy Walker,
Mayor of New York
until 1929

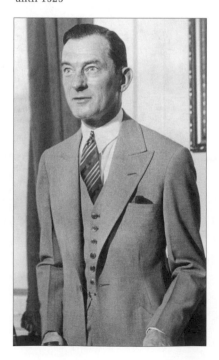

Billingsley with money provided by Frank Costello. The Stork Club, in which the famous columnist Walter Winchell sat to observe the scene every night of the week, was only ever closed once in its entire history—and this was one more time than MacSorley's saloon in Greenwich Village, which was a favourite watering-hole of police and politicians. MacSorley's didn't even pretend to change its famous beer to the permitted 'near' beer. It just kept on doing what it had always done, right out in the open.

What New York City had too, of course, was 17,000 policemen, backed up by 3,000 state police, 113 supreme court judges and 62 county prosecutors. It also had federal agencies, not to mention Prohibition agents by the hundreds. But so corrupted was the whole system of law enforcement by the huge amount of money made by bootleggers and speakeasy-operators that successful prosecutions against any of the big players were extremely rare. In any case, no support at all came from the Mayor's office, which was occupied until 1929 by the Tammany Hall fixer and ward-heeler *par excellence*, Jimmy Walker, and precious little was available from the State Governor, Al Smith, who thought Prohibition was a nonsense and often said as much.

The result was that everyone got into the act, an act that was being increasingly controlled by what was to become the New York version of Cosa Nostra. Longshoremen, fishermen, cops, judges and cabdrivers all got to dip their beaks: not only into the liquor it provided, but also into the deep lake of money that soon spilled over the banks of all propriety. Lucky Luciano later boasted of the bankers he knew of, the fancy parties he was asked to at the Whitneys' Long Island estate, and of the black-market tickets to the 1923 Jack Dempsey-Luis Angel Firpo fight that he provided to all his posh society friends. At the same time, he said later, he not only controlled every single police precinct in the City, but also had his bagman personally deliver $20,000 a month to Police Commissioner Grover A. Whelan. When Whelan was badly hurt by the Wall Street crash, Frank Costello loaned him $35,000 just to tide him over.

There were some small benefits that arrived in New York—and elsewhere—as a result of Prohibition: the fact that women were welcomed to speakeasies after being largely barred from saloons, and the discovery of the cocktail, invented to disguise the often foul taste of the alcohol available. But the minuses far outweighed the pluses and the biggest minus of them all was that America, in a sense, lost its innocence. Defying the law under Prohibition became fashionable for students, for flappers, for the respectable middle classes, as an expression of personal freedom, while the mobsters behind the scenes who provided the means to defy the law became, in effect, romantic heroes. There was a collusion, in other words, not only between crime and politics, but crime and society itself. Prohibition, as critic Karl Kraus once said about psychoanalysis, turned out to be the disease of which it purported to be the cure. This might have been a lesson that America could have taken into its future international campaigns, against communism and against drugs, but it was never learnt. And the Mafia again proved the beneficiary.

Al Smith, State Governor, was opposed to Prohibition and did little to help the authorities catch bootleggers

The Battle for Control: The New York Commission

Prohibition also had one further effect. With everyone's attention, up to highest national level, on booze, the Mafia was allowed by and large to get on with its business as usual: spreading its tentacles deeper and deeper into the trade unions and produce markets, into construction, gambling, slot-machines, prostitution and, for the first time, dope (the possibilities of dope may have first been suggested by Arnold Rothstein). There was little interference from the police—and, as for the federal agencies, even the Customs Service, which was highly active in New York State, never managed to uncover more than about five percent of the booze that poured over the border with Canada and out of the rum-runners' boats off-shore—about the same record the combined federal agencies have today with cocaine and heroin.

The only real threat, in fact, came from other gangs, from competitors in the free-for-all that was

Lucky Luciano would have to secure the support of the Sicilians to unite the warring New York gangs

Prohibition. Trucks were regularly hijacked, ship-ments were stolen and patches invaded. These were people, after all, playing for huge stakes, and there were plenty of young hoods on the look out for a bigger share of the profits. There just wasn't any discipline and the more mayhem there was, the worse it became for the common enterprise, since both police and politicians were duty-bound to sit up and take some notice at any rate.

It was because of this that Lansky and Luciano, together with their friend Vito Genovese, decided to launch a grand strategy aimed at bringing the warring gangs of New York together under a unified command. But first they had to create a power-base of their own which they could bring to the negotiat-ing table. Lansky probably had enough clout by now as a behind-the-scenes manipulator to bring the Jewish gangs onside. But Luciano had to secure the Sicilians.

Luciano and the 'Moustache Petes'

The two most powerful Sicilian bosses in New York during the 1920s were two old-style Mafia dons, Giuseppe Masseria and Salvatore Maranzano. They had always been rivals and Luciano, as a Masseria soldier, or perhaps *consigliere*, soon found himself inevitably involved. For all his status—or perhaps because of it—Maranzano decided both to teach him a lesson the old Sicilian way and to induce him to change his allegiance. Luciano was picked up, strung up by his thumbs from the ceiling and then tortured. Maranzano himself slashed him across the face with a knife, a wound that needed fifty-five stitches and left one side of Luciano's face permanently drooping. He was 'lucky' to have lived. He was finally let go, but by then Maranzano

Joseph Kennedy
was a source of
business inspira-
tion for Lansky and
Luciano

had exacted his price: the murder of Masseria in return for the number two spot in the Maranzano family.

Masseria was subsequently gunned down in the middle of dinner in a Coney Island restaurant, after Luciano, his dining partner, had left for the bathroom. Maranzano proclaimed himself the *capo di tutti capi* of the New York Sicilian families. Luciano, Lansky and Genovese, though, had other ideas. And a few months later in 1931, four of their men, posing as internal-revenue investigators, arrived at Maranzano's Park Avenue headquarters, demanding to see both the boss and the books. Maranzano was stabbed and shot to death in his inner office.

In victory, Luciano and Lansky took over Maranzano's idea. They brought order and central control to what became known as 'the five New York families'. But instead of making anyone the *capo di tutti capi*, they established a board of directors, the New York Commission—sometimes known as the National Crime Syndicate—and, together with it, an enforcement arm which came to be called Murder Incorporated. Luciano in this was the first among equals. It was he, above all, who took the now unified Mafia, both Jewish and Italian, into a whole new era. An associate later said of Luciano and Lansky: 'If they had been President and Vice-President of the United States, they would have run the place far better than the idiot politicians.'

They had almost certainly learned a lot by this time from the foreign banks and trading-houses which had helped finance the shipments of booze that had fed Prohibition America. They may also have learned from Joseph Kennedy, the father of President John Kennedy, how he concealed his

occasional forays into rum-running behind a pro-
tective shell of companies. But between them,
Lansky—whose first love remained the casinos he'd
seen as a young man with his boss Arnold
Rothstein—and Luciano, who after the War became
the American Mafia's representative in Europe, did
more to expand the New York mobs' reach and
influence across the United States and beyond than
anyone else. It was Luciano who first shifted the
Mafia into drugs. And it was Lansky, the grand
strategist, who moved the Mafia's money and
power into Las Vegas, movies and legitimate businesses all across the country. Lansky said in the
1970s (and only he perhaps really knew): 'We're
bigger than US Steel.'

11

The End of Prohibition and the Beginning of a New Era

New York Mayor Fiorello La Guardia sends a message to Dutch Shultz warning him not to bring back his gambling empire

P ROHIBITION finally came to an end in 1933 and it is instructive that many of Prohibition's major players immediately went into legitimate business in precisely the commodity out of which they'd made such huge amounts of money.

Joseph Kennedy became the American distributor of Haig & Haig Whisky and Gordon's Gin, Frank Costello set up Alliance Distributors, selling the same brands he'd made popular illegally. Samuel Bronfman, the biggest Canadian bootlegger, founded a company called Seagrams, and Luciano, Lansky and one of their torpedoes, Benjamin 'Bugsy' Siegel, started up Capitol Wine and Spirits, which specialised in top-end-of-the-market wines and liqueurs.

The Mafia, or Cosa Nostra, identified for the first time in 1984 by the aforementioned Sicilian don Tommaso Buscetta—went on, of course, to many other things. But the best way to tell this part of the organization's history is to go both backward and forward, and look at the careers of a number of the men who helped create the all-important

Did President
Roosevelt double
cross Lucky
Luciano?

Commission and its body of enforcers, Murder Incorporated: Dutch Schultz, Louis Lepke, Alberto Anastasia, Bugsy Siegel and Meyer Lansky himself.

As for Lucky Luciano, who used to have breakfast with Lansky at a delicatessen on Delancy Street every day he could, he was jailed in 1936 on a trumped-up charge of racketeering in prostitutes, and was put out of circulation in Sing Sing prison. He later said that he'd been double-crossed by President Roosevelt, for whom he'd brought out the vote in 1935. Roosevelt, through an intermediary, had offered to rein in, on Luciano's behalf, the investigations of Judge Samuel Seabury. He didn't. As President, he encouraged them further, and Luciano became his number-one victim. He was sentenced to between thirty and fifty years in prison. But his finest hour was yet to come.

Dutch Schultz

'Dutch' Schultz wasn't Dutch at all—he was German; and his last name wasn't Schultz—it was Flegenheimer. His father kept a saloon and livery-stable in what was known as Jewish Harlem, but deserted his family in 1916, and that was enough for son Arthur. After coming out of jail at the age of sixteen, from an eighteen-month stretch for burglary, he borrowed the name of a legendary member of the old Frog Hollow Gang, and got down to business.

A chorus girl once said that he looked like Bing Crosby with his face bashed in. Dutch certainly was no beauty, but then he didn't have to be. By the mid Twenties, after riding shotgun on Arnold Rothstein's liquor-trucks, he'd put together the toughest gang in New York, mainly operating in the

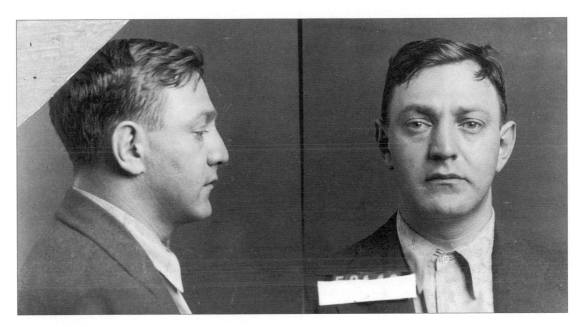

Dutch Schultz—a chorus girl once said he looked like Bing Crosby with his face bashed in

Bronx. They ran protection for some of the fanciest uptown restaurants. They were into slot machines and the numbers racket; liquor, restaurants, labour unions, gambling, and fixing any horse-race or box-ing-match they could. By the beginning of the Thirties, Dutch, who had a reputation for miserli-ness, was said to be making $20 million a year.

He didn't get to the top by any subtlety. He simply beat up or got rid of anyone who stood in his way. He out-muscled his competition—he arrived in the numbers racket, for example, by simply calling a meeting, laying his .45 on the table and saying 'I'm your partner.' When 'Legs' Diamond had to get out of New York after killing a drunk, Dutch took over his liquor trucks and then, when Legs objected, had him killed.

He avoided arrest in the usual way, by paying off the police and providing campaign funds and votes to all the politicians who mattered—particularly district attorney William Copeland Dodge. But a noose of prosecutions gradually settled round his

Special prosecutor
Thomas Dewey
tried to convict
Schultz on a tax
evasion charge in
1935

neck. He beat the rap on a tax-evasion charge in Syracuse in 1933, but in 1935 he faced another, this time put together by special prosecutor Thomas Dewey. His lawyers eventually succeeded in having the trial moved to a little upstate town, but the consensus was, in Lucky Luciano's words, that 'the loudmouth is never coming back.'

Schultz, though, spent months in tiny Malone, New York, before the trial, schmoozing the inhabitants, dressing modestly and even converting to Catholicism in the town's little church. When he got off, he told reporters: 'This tough world ain't no place for dunces. And you can tell all those smart guys in New York that the Dutchman is no dunce.'

The 'smart guys in New York', though, didn't want the Dutchman on their turf any more. Fiorello La Guardia, who'd succeeded Jimmy Walker as New York's Mayor, sent a message warning him not to come back, and started literally breaking up his gambling empire—he had himself photographed on barges taking a sledgehammer to Dutch's slot-machines. Thomas Dewey started preparing another case, this time against his restaurant rackets. His operation began to leak at the seams as other mobsters moved in on it.

He was exiled to Newark, New Jersey, where he set up his headquarters in a restaurant called the Palace Chop House. Then, sometime in late autumn 1935—after having had to kill one of his own lieutenants for conspiring with Luciano—he called a meeting of the Syndicate and demanded the assassination of Thomas Dewey. The Syndicate refused: it was far too high-profile. He said, fine, he'd kill Dewey himself—and so signed his own death warrant. In October, with his lieutenants, he was gunned down in the Palace Chop House by assassins from Murder Incorporated. He was thirty-three.

Louis Lepke

Louis Lepke, short for 'Lepkele' or 'Little Louis', was born Louis Buchalter in Williamsburg, Brooklyn in 1897. His father, the owner of a hardware store on the Lower East Side, died of a heart attack when he was thirteen, and his mother moved soon afterwards to Colorado. Little Louis, then, came of age in the streets. He hung out with hood-

Louis Buchalter—more commonly known as Louis Lepke, Lepkele or Little Louis

lums, and was soon in trouble with the law. He was sent out of town to live with his uncle in Connecticut, and then to a reformatory, from where he soon graduated, around the time of his twenty-first birthday, first to New York's Tombs prison, and then to Sing Sing, where he acquired the nickname 'Judge Louis'.

Back on the streets again in 1923, he went into the protection business with an old pal, Joseph 'Gurrah' Shapiro—they were known as 'the Gorilla Boys' and specialised in bakeries. But they didn't hit the big time until they went to work for Arnold Rothstein, who dealt large in both liquor and drugs—or so it was said. Soon they were were moving into the union rackets, backing the workers against the bosses with goon squads, and *vice versa*—and then taking over from both. They started out in this with a real expert, 'Little Augie' Orgen, as their principal mentor. But by 1927, Orgen simply stood in their way. So on October 15, they gunned him down in front of his clubhouse. By the beginning of the Thirties they ruled the labour roost. They controlled painters, truckers and motion-picture operators, they were expanding their drugs business and they still took in $1.5 million a year from bakeries. They were now known, not as 'the Gorilla Boys', but 'the Gold Dust Twins'.

In 1933, with the setting up of the Syndicate, Lepke became a board-director and one of the founding members of Murder Incorporated, its enforcement arm of contract-killers, among whom was a Brooklyn thug called Abraham 'Kid Twist' Reles. That same year, though, Lepke was indicted by a federal grand jury for violation of anti-trust laws. And though he ultimately beat the rap on this one, the Feds began closing in with narcotics charges, and the Brooklyn DA's office, with an

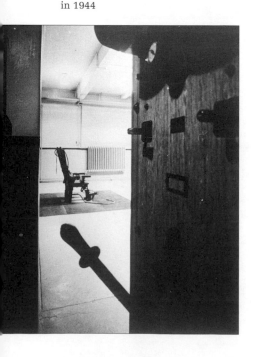

Lepke met his maker via the electric chair in 1944

investigation into racketeering. In the summer of 1937, he, along with 'Gurrah' Shapiro, went on the run, and soon became the most wanted man in US history.

While he was hiding he made attempts to silence the potential witnesses against him, but the heat on the streets became too great. In August 1940 he gave himself up, with the understanding that he'd face federal narcotics charges rather than a state indictment for murder. He was sentenced to fourteen years and shipped to the penitentiary at Leavenworth, Kansas.

Then, though, Abe Reles, 'Kid Twist', one of the executioners he'd hired in the old days, began to sing. For six months Reles was held at a hotel in Coney Island as he gave evidence at trial after trial. On November 12, 1941, his body was found—apparently he'd jumped from a sixth-storey window—but it was too late for Louis Lepke. Reles had already appeared before a grand-jury hearing to give evidence against him, evidence that could be—and was—used in court.

Louis Lepke and two of his lieutenants, Mendy Weiss and Louis Capone, were tried for murder and condemned to death. They went to the electric chair in Sing Sing prison on March 4, 1944. The murder of Reles—which got Alberto Anastasia and Bugsy Siegel off the hook—was probably arranged by Frank Costello.

Alberto Anastasia

Alberto Anastasia seems to have arrived in New York from Sicily as an illegal immigrant during the First World War. But he was soon cutting his criminal teeth—like so many other future Mafia leaders—in the gang of 'Little Augie' Orgen.

Alberto Anastasia
began his mob life
in the gang of Little
Augie Orgen

Orgen's assassination by Lepke's men in 1927 split the gang into factions, and Anastasia soon threw in his lot with the three men who were to reshape and reorganize the Mafia on a national basis: Meyer Lansky, Vito Genovese and Lucky Luciano. He became one of their strong-arms and hit-men, alongside Bugsy Siegel. And when the New York Commission— or National Criminal Syndicate—was finally set up, he became one of the two founding fathers of its enforcement arm, taking responsibility for long-distance contract killings.

In 1940, though, Abe Reles, one of his killers-for-hire, turned stoolie and started giving detailed evidence about dozens of murders in which Anastasia had been implicated. He went underground and only re-emerged in November 1941 when Reles had his unfortunate 'accident', falling to his death from the hotel in which the Brooklyn DA had hidden him, under supposed police protection.

No-one was ever charged in Reles' death. But the case against Anastasia, with him out of the way, collapsed and he was free to play his part, after the

Did Vito Genovese order the killing of Anastasia because he was invading his turf?

Joe Valachi, one of history's very rare Mafia witnesses. It was through his testimonies that many of the Mafia's inner workings were first revealed

War and the exile of Lucky Luciano to Italy, in the mob battles for control of Luciano's gambling and drugs operations in the US. He emerged as head of the Mangano family. But his style of doing business—and his increasing ambition—didn't sit well with the bosses of the other clans. So on October 25, 1957, when Anastasia went down to the basement barber's shop in Manhattan's Park-Sheraton Hotel for his regular haircut, two men followed him and shot him to death with automatic pistols as he sat in the barber's chair. Then they threw down their weapons, went back up to street-level and disappeared.

Eight years later, a Mafia soldier called Joe Valachi claimed that the killing had been ordered by Anastasia's old associate, Vito Genovese, on the grounds that Anastasia had been invading his turf. The members of the Commission had agreed. In the old days, of course, at this point they would have got in touch with Murder Incorporated—and Alberto Anastasia himself.

Valachi—one of that vanishingly rare species, a Mafia witness—also revealed for the first time two things about the American Cosa Nostra: first, that the *capi* themselves had no direct involvement in crime of any kind, but only through intermediaries; and second, that its profits were already by that time being laundered through legitimate businesses.

Benjamin 'Bugsy' Siegel

Bugsy Siegel was there right at the beginning of the new-look New York Mafia. He was in the jail-cell, so one of the stories went, where Lucky Luciano first got together with Meyer Lansky. He was one of the four gunmen who murdered Giuseppe Masseria

Bugsy Siegel, the founding father of Las Vegas

Clark Gable and Jean Harlow were both to be found frequenting Siegel's Vegas establishments

and one of the four 'internal-revenue agents' who were in at the kill of Salvatore Maranzano, the ruthless would-be *capo di tutti capi* of the city's underworld. He was also appointed, along with Meyer Lansky, to the board of the Unione Siciliana, one of the first attempts at a commission to guide the power of the Mafia nation-wide. He may not have understood much about the politics—he started out as a small-time car-thief and driver of booze-trucks, after all—and he left that sort of

Casinos had always been popular during Prohibition, but in Vegas they became legitimate business enterprises

thing, in any case, to Luciano and Lansky. But he knew all the right people. He was presentable, and in 1935 he must have seemed the ideal choice to spearhead the New York families' expansion of

Howard Hughes
reportedly
bankrolled much
of Siegel's casino,
The Flamingo

operations to the West Coast.

Teaming up in southern California with a local mob led by Jack Dragna, Siegel ran drugs and operated a string of gambling-clubs and offshore casino-ships on behalf of his New York bosses both before and during the War. With the help of his pal, actor George Raft—and with his rough edges smoothed off by a divorced millionairess called Countess Dorothy Di Frasso— he was at ease in the best Hollywood circles. He was on first-name terms with people like Jean Harlow, Clark Gable and Gary Cooper—and a magnet to every starlet. He fitted right in.

Gambling and stars: it was this combination that was to lead to Siegel's one major contribution to Mafia history. In 1945, he suggested to his bosses the idea of building a casino and hotel in the Nevada desert at a place called Las Vegas. He put together $3 million, some of it reportedly from Howard Hughes, and the Commission soon organized a loan to match his investment. The place, he said, would be called The Flamingo—a name suggested by his girlfriend Virginia Hill. There would be a grand opening, with all of Hollywood's royalty there.

However, word soon got back to the centre that money was disappearing during The Flamingo's building, some of it salted away abroad and a decision was taken at an informal meeting of bosses in Havana, Cuba, that Siegel would have to repay with interest the East-Coast Mafia investment as soon as the hotel-casino opened. Trouble was, the grand opening that Siegel had planned turned out a disaster. Bad weather kept planes grounded at LA airport and the stars never showed. In two weeks, The Flamingo was closed after losing $100,000.

Bugsy couldn't pay, and his old friends in New York could no longer protect him. It was a matter of business; an example had to be set. So on the night of June 20, 1947, Siegel was gunned down as he sat in the living-room of Virginia Hill's Los Angeles house on North Linden Drive. The final bullet, the 'calling card', was fired into his left eye. Just five people came to his funeral.

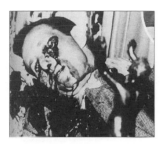

June 20, 1947: Bugsy Siegel is killed in Los Angeles

The Flamingo started up again not long after under new management. It was soon followed by two more Las Vegas casinos, the Tropicana, controlled by Frank Costello, and the Thunderbird, controlled by Meyer Lansky.

Meyer Lansky and the Aftermath

Lansky and Luciano are often said to be the instigators of the Mafia's move into drugs

One of the problems with writing about the Mafia in America is that it was described for decades as non-existent, a mirage. So the roots, for example, of the trade in heroin and cocaine in which the United States and many other Western countries are now enmeshed, remain buried, out of sight, though there is a general view today that it was Lansky and Luciano that set the Mafia down this road in an organized way. It is said that Lansky himself became hooked on heroin after his son was born crippled, and then did cold turkey in a hideout in Massachusetts, watched over by a hood called Vincent 'Jimmy Blue Eyes' Alo, ever after a close friend.

After that, though—and after Luciano's imprisonment—Lansky more and more took to the shadows, living apparently quietly in a tract house in Miami, as he moved the Mafia into gambling operations in Las Vegas, the Bahamas and Cuba.

In 1970, after hearing that he faced tax-evasion charges, Lansky, by now sixty-eight, fled to a hotel he owned in Tel Aviv, before being extradited, by order of the Israeli Supreme Court, back to the US. In the end, he was acquitted. In the late Seventies and early Eighties he could be seen walking his dog along Miami's Collins Avenue or else having a meal in a diner with his old friend 'Jimmy Blue Eyes'. He died from a heart attack in 1983, at the age of eighty-one.

Lansky was the last of his kind and by now the Jewish mobs were a thing of the past. The Jews, like the Irish and German waves of immigrants before them, had passed into the mainstream. Only the Sicilians, the five families set up by Lansky and Luciano remained: the Genoveses, the Gambinos, the Luccheses, the Bonannos and the Colombos. They remained, at least in part, because they retained close ties with the island from which they derived: the last great redoubt of the Mafia and the site of its rebirth: Sicily.

*

More perhaps than any other single man, Lucky Luciano created the modern face of the Mafia: making vast profits from drugs, operating across borders, invisible, bolstered by international agreements and alliances and ruled by representative councils.

It wasn't long, however, before they outgrew Orgen's gang and looked for new opportunities, together with a friend of Luciano's called Vito Genovese. Prohibition made the three of them increasingly powerful. Luciano later claimed that he personally controlled every New York police precinct and had a bagman deliver $20,000 a month to Police Commissioner Grover A. Whelan. He also boasted about the company he moved in: the politicians and stars he met at parties and the gatherings at the Whitney estate. The politicians, even presidential candidates, courted him for campaign funding and help at election time. The beautiful people wooed him for World Series baseball tickets, girls, dope and drink.

However, there remained one major obstacle to Luciano's assumption of absolute power. The most important criminal power-brokers in New York, even during Prohibition, were two old-style Mafia bosses, and he would need to break with the old ways if he was to achieve absolute power and control.

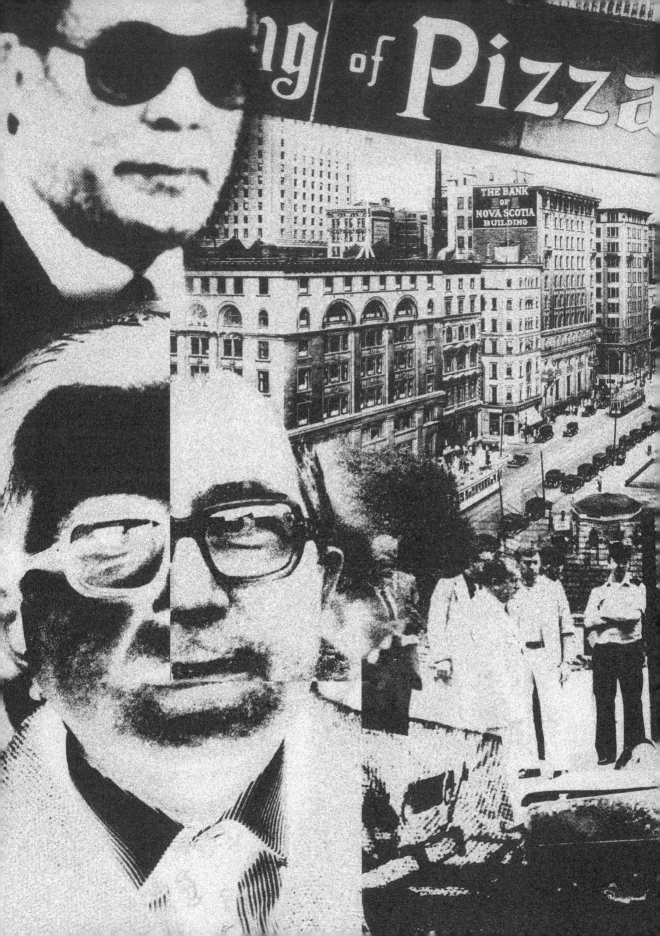

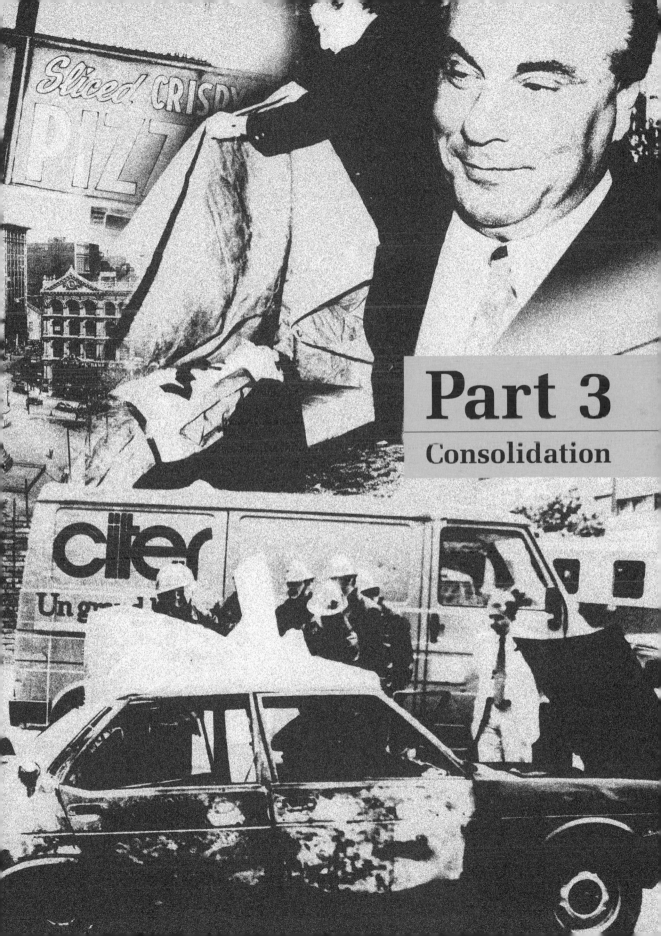

Part 3

Consolidation

12

Lucky Luciano, Don Calò and the Invasion of Sicily

L UCKY LUCIANO was about to stage the greatest coup of his life, and from an unlikely place: his cell in Sing Sing Prison. When the United States entered the Second World War against the Axis powers—one of them Italy—immigrant Italians soon found themselves with divided loyalties. There was sabotage in the New York docks where many of them worked, interruption and theft of war supplies, and spying. Officers of US naval intelligence, knowing that the ultimate authority in the docks belonged to the Mafia through its control of the longshoremen's unions, then approached Luciano to co-opt his help. Luciano obliged. From then on, on his say-so, the sabotage and the delays stopped. The war effort went on unimpeded.

However, Luciano had another service to offer his new friends. Word began to go out to immigrants from Sicily to help the authorities—to identify for them the best places to land on the island, the nature of the ground that would have to be traversed by any invading army and the safest paths and routes. Messages were also sent in Luciano's

Mussolini brutally
put down the
Sicilian Mafia
during his twenty-
year reign

name to key figures in the Sicilian Mafia, instructing them to co-operate with the Americans when they arrived. Fully five months before the final landing, Luciano—who'd been born Salvatore Lucania near Villalba—launched an appeal against his thirty-to-fifty-year sentence for prostitution-running on the grounds of 'services rendered to the nation'.

Though Luciano was not yet to get out of prison, everything went according to his master-plan. When American forces landed in central and western Sicily in early July 1943, fifteen percent of the soldiers were of Sicilian birth or descent. They carried with them not only the American flag, but others emblazoned with the letter 'L' for Luciano. These soon appeared all over the island as the Americans advanced with the help of expert Mafia guides—one was even dropped, it is said, from a reconnaissance plane at the doorstep of the priest in Villalba, who just happened to be the brother of the island's *capo di tutti capi*, Don Calogero Vizzini.

Ten days after the landing, Don Calò was picked up behind the lines in Villalba by American tanks and whisked away. He was made an honorary colonel in the US Army, but became known to the footsoldiers as 'General Mafia'.

Don Calò played his part well. The Sicilian Mafia had for twenty years been brutally put down by Mussolini, so they could be shown to the naive Americans to be demonstrably 'anti-fascist'. They were released at his behest from Mussolini's jails as the Americans advanced and installed in top positions in almost every municipality under the military administration they left in their wake. Don Calò and other Mafia bosses had lists of fascist sympathisers and collaborators with the Germans in their areas. Communists were clearly unacceptable. Who else, after all, was there to trust but the fellow freedom-fighters who had prepared the ground and cleared the passes for their American liberators?

With Don Calò at their side, encouraging Italian soldiers to desert, it took the American force just seven days to conquer central and western Sicily. General Patton called it 'the fastest blitzkrieg in history'. There were negligible casualties, as the Italian army seemed to melt away from their positions alongside the Germans. The British, under General Montgomery, were not so fortunate. It took them five weeks to battle their way up the island's east coast, with thousands of losses.

Vito Genovese and the Spoils of War

Vito Genovese— confederate and friend to Lucky Luciano and Meyer Lansky

When the Allies went on to the mainland of Italy, they were soon met by another Mafia representative, Vito Genovese. Genovese had escaped to Italy from New York in 1937, on the run from a murder charge and had become a close friend of Mussolini. He'd made major donations to the Fascist Party and had been awarded the title of *Commendatore*, one of Italy's highest honours. He'd also, so it was said, generously provided Mussolini's son with cocaine and organized the killing of a New York anti-fascist newspaper editor through the good offices of Carmine Galante.

With the Allies headed towards Rome, though, Genovese quickly saw the light and he reappeared as the official interpreter and adviser to the US military governor of Naples, Colonel Charles Peretti, who was already, Lucky Luciano was later to say laconically, 'a good friend'. He proved an invaluable fixer, particularly to a group of senior American officers, through whom he bribed his

Vito Genovese was
finally arrested in
Missouri in 1958
on drugs and
smuggling charges.
He died in prison
eleven years later

way into the black market. Soon sixty percent of all food unloaded by the Allies in the port was disappearing into the hands of Genovese's network of corrupt American soldiers and local Camorra men, and though Genovese was shipped back to the US in 1944, by that time he had already paid more than one visit to Sicily with Colonel Peretti to see Don Calò. His network in Naples, furthermore, remained in place—to be taken over by Lucky Luciano when, finally released from his American prison and deported, he settled in Naples in 1948.

Sicily: The Battle against the Communists

The aftermath of
the Second World
War saw the com-
munists gaining
more influence
in Sicily

With Sicily now under Allied control, there were headaches for the military government—and for the landowners who as ever ruthlessly controlled for their own benefit both the land and the rural poor. In the cities there were food riots, and in the countryside demonstrations for land reform. Meanwhile, in the north—and to a degree in Sicily—the communists had emerged from under cover after their long battle against fascism and were entering politics as an organized force for the first time. The Christian Democratic Party, founded with a ringing endorsement from the Pope and hidden backing from the Americans, were not yet the strong bastion against them that they were to become.

The landowners, then, needed help, and so did

Food riots and
demonstrations
over land reform
saw the authorities
on full alert in 1946

the military government. And it was in this atmosphere that they both turned, once more, to the
Mafia, who were not only anti-communist in precisely the way the military government demanded,
but were also by now dreaming—as were huge
numbers of Sicilians—of separation from Italy, of
becoming a British colony or America's forty-ninth
state.

In September 1944, Don Calò demonstrated the
Mafia's credentials as solidly anti-communist when
his men bombed and shot up a joint communist
and socialist meeting in Villalba he had himself
permitted 'as long as neither the Mafia nor land
reform were discussed'. Within two months, the US
consul in Palermo was secretly reporting to his
boss, US Secretary of State Cordell Hull, that Don
Calò was having meetings with both military and
Mafia figures about nominating a Mafia boss as the
head of an insurrectionary separatist movement.

In the end, the movement, which at its height
had over half a million supporters, fizzled out.
Early in 1946, even before the new Italian constitu-
tion had been approved, the provisional
government announced that it was giving Sicily a
high degree of autonomy: its own elected parliament, the right to collect its own taxes and control
over the money that from then on—and for thirty
years into the future—was to flow to it from Rome.
This was an offer the Mafia simply could not
refuse: money, and plenty of it, in return for votes.
It already had gathering control over local politics
and the beginnings of a deal with the Christian
Democrats. But if separatism died in the hearts of
men like Don Calò, anti-communism did not, particularly in one of the most enigmatic characters of
modern Sicilian history, Salvatore Giuliano.

Salvatore Giuliano

The Sicilian bandit
Salvatore Giuliano

Salvatore Giuliano was a bandit. A peasant from Montelepre, he had killed a *carabiniere* in 1943 at the age of twenty, when stopped by a patrol while carrying contraband grain. Four months later he killed another during a police raid and a few weeks later he organized a prison breakout which was to form the basis of his gang. There were many gangs like Giuliano's in Sicily at the time, and most of them were quickly put down. But Giuliano's survived and became famous, mostly because of his daring and charm. Known as 'the King of Montelepre', he played host to the national and international press. He dispensed popular justice, he was flamboyant and handsome and he even had a brief fling with a Swedish photojournalist. He was also mysteriously well connected. He met with the chief prosecutor of Palermo and with Vito Genovese during one of his visits. He had contacts with police and politicians. It remains to many a mystery how he could have survived for the seven years he did after that first killing of his—unless it was in the interests of some very powerful people to keep him alive.

One group of powerful people was almost certainly the Mafia. For in the brief insurrectionary period of the separatist movement Giuliano was made a colonel in the separationists' army, probably at the request of Don Calò. He was also a strong anti-communist, and that suited the Americans' purposes well. In addition to robbing the rich—he once took a diamond ring off the duchess of Pratameno's finger in her Palermo *palazzo*—he also raided and firebombed the offices of what he called 'the vile reds'. So it must have been among his worst nightmares—as well as those of the Mafia, who were quietly moving into an alliance with the American-backed Christian

President Truman
announced Italy
was in the front line
against the threat of
communism

There were many
gangs like Giuliano's in
Sicily in the 1940s,
and most of them were
quickly put down

Democrats—when, in the first elections for the new
Sicilian parliament in April 1947, the United Left—
not the Christian Democrats—won.

Giuliano had already written to US President
Truman about the need 'to stem the communist tide
in Sicily' and Truman had, in effect, agreed, by
announcing that Italy was in the front line of the
battle against this world threat. Bandit and president, in other words, were of one mind. On May 1,
1947, Truman's secretary of state, George Marshall,
wrote to the US ambassador, saying that the com-

munists should be excluded from the national government, and on the same day Giuliano killed as many of them as he could find.

Still nothing is known for certain about what came to be called the massacre at Portella della Ginestra. The documents relating to it have never been published, and an Italian senator who saw them declared it would cause 'a national catastrophe if they ever came to light'. All that is known is that when 1500 or so villagers met in an open space outside Piana to celebrate May Day, Giuliano's men opened up on them from the flanks of a mountain above, killing 11 and wounding 65. There were rumours that they were armed with the latest American weapons and even that some of the men were dressed in American uniforms. But as to who gave the order for the massacre, it is—in the words of a 1972 parliamentary commission—'absolutely impossible to attribute responsibility either directly or morally to this or that party or politician.'

After the massacre, though, Giuliano's local usefulness seems to have come to an end and most of his gang were one by one caught and disposed of— several of them, according to the writer Norman Lewis, 'being added to the scrupulously kept list of those—now amounting to over five hundred names—who had slipped on the stairs of the Ucciardone prison.' By June 1950, Giuliano was alone, except for his cousin and right hand Gaspare Pisciotta. There was said to have been an offer of amnesty for both men, even of an American military plane to fly them away to the United States. But on July 4, in a Mafia safe house in Castelvetrano—where Giuliano, by report, spent his time reading Shakespeare and Descartes—he was shot dead by his cousin as he lay sleeping.

Immediately a cover-up began. Giuliano's body

was taken outside by the *carabinieri* and pumped full of bullets as if he'd died in combat. By the time the world's press arrived, a fog of lies already surrounded the death, including one suggestion, faithfully reported, that some 350 men of the newly set-up Banditry Suppression Taskforce Command had been involved. This scenario, however, soon fell apart. For one thing, the blood from Giuliano's body seemed to have run uphill from his corpse and for another, Pisciotta proved all too ready to claim responsibility.

In the end, for all the attempted cover-up, Pisciotta was charged with Giuliano's murder and put on trial in Viterbo on the mainland, where he announced early in the trial that he'd killed

The Banditry Suppression Taskforce Command—claimed by many to have been involved in Giuliano's death

Giuliano at the request of Italian Minister of the
Interior Scelba who, with a group of landowners,
had also been behind the massacre at Portella della
Ginestre. He said that later he'd reveal all. But he
was not to have the chance. He died of poison in
Ucciardone prison on January 8, 1954—the same
day that Christian Democrat Scelba was sworn in as
Prime Minister of Italy.

13

The Mafia at Corleone

DON CALO DIED of a heart attack in early 1952, and with his death there began to ebb away for ever the old rural traditions of the Sicilian Mafia, which had always been more concerned with power and influence than with money. Though the title of *capo di tutti capi* passed to his successor in Villalba, Giuseppe Genco Russo, the future increasingly belonged to men like Luciano Liggio and Totò Riina, young killers from Corleone who'd learned a new attitude from those American gangsters who'd either stayed in or returned to Sicily after the War. Liggio, the senior of the two men, was an estate-manager and hit-man for his boss in Corleone, Dr Michele Navarra. Both had been implicated in 1948 in the murder of a brave young trade unionist and labour organizer called Placido Rizzotto, who had disappeared soon after the 1947 election. Rizzotto had somehow contrived to win the local council for the left, despite Navarra's attempts to rig the poll by issuing several hundred certificates for blindness or extreme myopia to local women, so that they would have to be accompanied to the voting station by his men. Retribution was swift. Rizzotto was taken at gun-point outside the town and hanged from a tree by Luciano Liggio. Then his body was thrown into a hundred-foot-deep crevasse. A shepherd-boy who'd reported what he'd seen was given something by the good Dr Navarra to calm his nerves—and promptly died.

Both Navarra and Liggio were later charged with the deaths, thanks mainly to a captain of *carabinieri* from northern Italy who'd been assigned to Corleone: a young man who was later to play a crucial role in the uncovering of post-war Mafia activities, Carlo Alberto Dalla Chiesa. Liggio was acquitted for lack of evidence and though Dr Navarra was sentenced to five years' exile in Calabria, he was—thanks to his friends in the Christian Democratic Party—welcomed back to Corleone after just a few months to the strains of the town band.

The End of the Old Ways

Cigarette smuggling became the new money-spinner for the Mafia in the post war years

By this time Lucky Luciano had set up his new home in Naples and he was quickly instrumental in bringing together Vito Genovese's old Camorra network and members of the Sicilian Mafia in what was to become one of their chief post-war money-spinners: cigarette-smuggling. The Italian government had awarded itself a monopoly on the sale and distribution of cigarettes, but the cigarettes almost everyone wanted were American—and the Mafia provided them, just as they'd provided the booze during Prohibition. Gross profits amounted, it was said, to at least $1 billion a year.

The other big money-spinner for the Sicilians was land-speculation and construction. With money pouring into the island from the mainland

The number of heroin addicts in America tripled after the war

and with building booming, it was child's play to find out from crooked politicians and bureaucrats which areas were due next to get planning permission. These would then be bought up wholesale at agricultural rates by building companies headed by Mafia front-men—front-men who weren't bothered at all by the quality of what they actually put up. The profits here were not as great as in cigarette smuggling, but they still amounted to well over $100 million a year.

The old businesses of the traditional Mafia went on, of course: protection rackets, grain smuggling and control over commodities in short supply. Dr Navarra started a bus company with the American military vehicles he was allowed to commandeer. Luciano Liggio seems to have made much of his living from butchering stolen cattle. But the future—and Liggio knew it—lay not in the countryside any more but in Palermo, where the politicians and the money were. The countryside was becoming increasingly poor and depopulated: between 1951 and 1953, 400,000 Sicilians emigrated to Australia, Argentina and elsewhere and there were no longer enough labourers to work many of the huge hereditary estates.

There was also an up-and-coming new business to get into: heroin. Luciano seems to have set up his first heroin-processing plant in Palermo in 1949, using morphine base smuggled in from the Lebanon. As the number of heroin addicts tripled in the United States, he was a regular visitor to the Sicilian capital. He was busily suggesting to those who would listen, not only a serious investment in the drugs trade, but also the setting-up of a central Commission, or *cupola*, of the sort he'd set up in America, to direct Mafia activities and keep the peace between factions. He wanted the Sicilians, in other words, to do two things based on the US experience: to go international, and to grow up.

Luciano Liggio and his right hand Totò Riina agreed. But first they had to create a power-base of their own in Corleone. So after an argument with Dr Navarra over involvement in a dam project, which would have made Liggio a fortune in protection and speculation, they killed him in 1958 after ambushing his car. They then set about exterminating, one by one, every member of his faction they could find. Between 1958 and 1963 the modest town of Corleone became one of the murder-capitals of the world.

One man, though, was watching: a man who was later to do more than anyone else to bring down the Mafia in Sicily. His name was Tommaso Buscetta, the highest Mafia figure ever to break the code of *omerta* and become a witness for the State. He had by now helped to set up the Commission Luciano had suggested, and he later said of Dr Navarra's murder that it was 'the underlying cause of the crisis that afflicted the Mafia organization [from then on].' By killing for personal gain, Liggio had set a precedent in which the Mafia's traditional codes of conduct stood for nothing. It was for Buscetta the beginning of the end.

Joe Bananas Visits Sicily

Liggio and Riina were playing for big stakes, though. The year before they killed Dr Navarra, at the height of a major war over control of Palermo's wholesale meat market, a visitor from the United

States had arrived, to be met like a visiting states-man at Rome airport, complete with a red carpet, by the Italian Minister for Foreign Trade, Bernardo Mattarella. This was apt enough, since Mattarella had grown up with his visitor in Castellamare del Golfo outside Palermo—and doubly apt, perhaps, in as much as a young Christian Democrat protégé of his, a 'made' Mafia man called Salvo Lima, was about to become Palermo's mayor. Giuseppe Bonanno, known as Joe Bananas, the head of one of New York's five families, was his visitor, and he was on his way to Palermo for a summit meeting with his Sicilian counterparts.

The meeting took place at the Grand Hotel et des Palmes in Palermo between October 10 and 14, 1957. The highpoint seems to have been a dinner hosted on the twelfth by Lucky Luciano at the Spano restaurant. The guestlist at the meeting and the dinner were slightly different, but Joe Bananas and his *consigliere* Carmine Galante, who super-vised a heroin network for the Bonanno family, were present at both. The subjects under discussion were the same: the setting up of the Sicilian Commission and the establishment of a heroin supply-and-sale network in which the Sicilians and the Americans would be equal partners. At the dinner, Luciano introduced the Americans to family boss Salvatore 'Ciaschiteddu' (Little Bird) Greco, his nominee for head of the Commission, and also to a group of young likelies, among them Tommaso Buscetta. At the meeting, three more heads of families were present, including Don Calò's successor as *capo di tutti capi*, Giuseppe Genco Russo. Both Buscetta and Liggio may also have been there.

Whoever attended the meeting, though, the upshot was the same: the establishment of the

Commission, under Salvatore Greco, was agreed and a joint partnership with the Bonanno family in the smuggling of heroin was cemented—subject to the agreement of a meeting of the New York Commission later in the year. Within a matter of weeks, as a gesture of good faith, untraceable Sicilian assassins had gunned down the brutal and stupid Alberto Anastasia, one of the founders of Murder Incorporated, in a New York city barber's chair. But the approval of the American Commission was not gained—at least not until later. The summit meeting in Appalachin, New York, due to address the matter, was raided by the police, and for the first time senior American Mafia figures were exposed.

Lucky Luciano decided that the project should go ahead anyway. In fact he had already begun it, with the establishment of the so-called French Connection.

The French Connection

One of Luciano's problems was that there was a lack of skilled chemists in Sicily and Naples. Both Sicilians and Neapolitans were expert smugglers—and there was never any problem with couriers to take the refined heroin into the United States, usually via Canada. But organizing a sophisticated chemical laboratory capable of turning morphine base into refined heroin was quite another matter. So Luciano had turned early on to the organization which controlled the docks at Marseilles, the secret Union Corse—and in so doing had taken hold of another present gifted to organized crime by the Americans.

At the end of the War, the Americans had faced exactly the same problem in France that they had

Opposite: The docks at Marseilles became the base for the French Connection

A case of the type
commonly used by
drug smugglers in
the Fifties

in Italy: i.e. the rise of the communists who—as in Italy—had fought with the socialists as partisans. Now there was a growing fear in America that the well-organized and increasingly popular communists would seize power in a coup d'état. So the CIA and the State Department decided to seize the bull by the horns and take them on in one of their most important strongholds: Marseilles.

Marseilles was the most important port in France, and its docks were controlled by communist-led unions who provoked civil unrest in the form of demonstrations and street battles. The CIA poured money and agents—including a psychological warfare team—into the city. They also recruited old allies in their fight against the communists, particularly among the Union Corse, many of whose members had been Resistance fighters and/or American agents.

One of the men they particularly turned to had been both. Antoine Guerini had worked as a contact man for both British and American intelligence, and had been an important conduit for the Allies' parachute-drops of arms. Now he was put in charge of a force of Corsican strong-arms handpicked by him, whose job it was to secure control of the docks for the socialists whom the CIA were backing. He was soon successful; and with control of the port now in his hands and an army of enforcers at his back, he went on to take over one of Marseilles' bigger businesses, the heroin trade.

How much connivance the CIA had in this is unknown. But Marseilles became, under Guerini and Luciano's aegis, one of the key links in the heroin trail that led from the Middle East through Sicily and then onward to the United States. The Sicilians provided the morphine-base and shipment to Marseilles. They also took care of the onward journey of refined heroin to America, where their American partners were in charge of distribution. Gigantic profits were generated along the way, enough for everyone to share in. Buying a kilo of morphine base might cost, say, $1000, but by the time it had been refined to ninety percent pure heroin and delivered to the US, that same kilo would have multiplied in value by over thirty times, and at street level, diluted with milk powder, it'd be worth fully $300,000 at early 1950s' prices. Value added in Marseilles, in other words $6000 a kilo; value added by successful arrival in New York: a further $23,000—for something that could be carried in a shopping bag several kilos at a time.

An American Drug Enforcement Agency officer, who worked in France at the height of the French

Connection, later remarked that in the late Sixties and early Seventies, 'it's no coincidence that we arrested over forty former French intelligence officers': i.e. men who'd been as useful to the French as they'd been to the Americans.

14

The Death and Legacy of Lucky Luciano

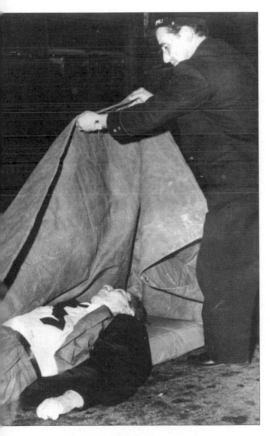

Lucky Luciano finally ran out of good fortune at Naples airport in 1962

IN 1962, the visionary Luciano died at Naples airport, waiting for the arrival of a Hollywood producer who wanted to make a film of his life. It is also said that there were Interpol agents there who wanted to interview him too. The official cause of death was a heart attack, but there were those who claimed that he was stricken after drinking a cup of coffee. So the possibility remains that he was poisoned, either because a film would bring his associates unwelcome publicity or because they were afraid of what he might say if arrested.

He'd left behind him, though, what was to prove an abiding legacy. All the ingredients that were to lead to the domination of the Sicilian Mafia over huge swathes of the Italian economy were now in place. Via its control over the countryside and over the water supply to orchards, it had moved into the island's slaughterhouses, produce markets and food-processing plants. It controlled the docks and the Palermo mayor's office. It took in perhaps thirty percent of all the money invested in the island's development by the central government; and its tentacles reached high into the Christian Democratic Party, for whom it regularly now delivered the all-important Sicilian vote. It was also in charge of almost all buildings in Palermo. Under Salvo Lima, by now a member of the Italian parliament, and his successor as mayor of Palermo, a Mafia ex-barber from Corleone called Vito Ciancimino, 2500 of 4000 building licences given between 1958 and 1964 went to just three people, all Mafia fronts.

It also had its Commission and, with heroin, what was to become an unending stream of money—money which could be housed in banks which, because of Sicilian autonomy, were not governed by Italy's central bank. It was also well on its way to control over Sicily's tax-gathering, much of which ended up in the hands of two cousins, Ignazio and Nino Salvo—and this wasn't small money either. The commission paid to Sicilian agents was ten percent of all the monies taken in, three times more than in the rest of the country.

The First Sicilian Mafia War

The potential pickings, then, were huge, and after the death of Luciano the Sicilian families viciously fought each other for them in what turned out to be the final struggle between the old style and the new. The new Mafiosi, among them Luciano Liggio, had probably been influenced by the American hoods who'd returned to Sicily as a result of pressure from Senator Estes Kefauver's Special Commission which in the early Fifties had established the existence of a nationwide crime syndicate in America known as the Mafia. They brought with them not only management techniques, but also lessons in gang warfare. The Sicilians were quick to catch on.

Part of the struggle was territorial. The terms and conditions under which the Sicilian Commission had been set up made it slightly different from its American counterpart. In New York, that's to say, the word 'territory' was used metaphorically. The waste-disposal business, for example, was seen as the 'territory' of the Gambino and Lucchese families, while the docks 'belonged' to the Genoveses. In Sicily, the division between families was much more geographically-based, centred on particular towns and villages and areas in Palermo. There were regional commissions that presided over each 'province', i.e. the territory of three contiguous families; and these in turn sent representatives to the central Cupola.

In theory, this should have worked. After all, the Sicilian Mafia was in the first place a cartel, an association of producers of a commodity called protection, and the commission's job was on the face of it simple: to discipline each of the individual producers of protection and to restrict competition from outsiders. But there were several problems with this. In the first place, these individual producers were not stable organizations. Luciano Liggio, for example, who was to make the Corleonesi a truly formidable power, was still blasting his way to control over the competition within his own territory.

Secondly, there were inequalities of opportunity, and these were exacerbated both by the building boom in Palermo and by the Mafia's new business of drugs. The Cinisi family, for example—led by Cesare Manzella and his deputy Gaetano Badalamenti—were centred on a seaside town on the way to Palermo airport. The airport was part of its territory and this gave them a vital edge in the smuggling of any contraband. The family of Angelo and Salvatore Barbera, meanwhile, controlled an area in Palermo full of new building. This gave them a major and much envied source of extra revenue which they were able to invest elsewhere, particularly in the new and all-important business of heroin.

As if this wasn't enough, there were inter-family deals that went wrong, investments that failed to pay off, amid a general atmosphere of secret suspicion. And the result was a gathering toll of punishment murders followed by killings in revenge: vendettas. In 1962 and early 1963, the heads of three Palermo families were killed, including Cesare Manzella and Salvatore Barbera. Angelo Barbera, on the run in Milan, was badly wounded. Finally, an attack made on the Greco family—headed by Salvatore 'Little Bird' Greco, the head of the Cupola—went badly wrong. A car bomb left outside the house of a trusted Greco lieutenant exploded while being examined—and seven soldiers and policemen were killed.

The result was a massive crackdown on the Mafia. There were arrests all over the island. Totò Riina was taken at the end of 1963, followed four months later by Luciano Liggio. So intense was police activity that the Cupola was suspended and many of the individual families dissolved. Salvatore Greco himself took refuge in Brazil. There were too few Mafia soldiers on the street—they were all in prison awaiting trial—to be able to do proper business.

In the end, two separate trials took place on the mainland: one relating to the five-year bloodbath in Corleone, and the other to the inter-family wars in Palermo. But the result in each was more or less the same. In the Palermo trial, which wound up in

The Palermo trial,
the result of a mas-
sive crackdown on
the Mafia in the
Sixties, saw 60 of
the 114 defendants
acquitted

The Corleone trial
saw all defendants
acquitted due to a
'lack of evidence'

December 1968, 60 of the 114 defendants were acquitted and most of the rest were found guilty only of minor charges. As for the Corleone trial, the judge and jury had been effectively softened up by threats of death, and all were acquitted the following year 'for lack of evidence'. The only significant aftermath was that Totò Riina was arrested again soon after his return to Corleone and exiled to a small town near Bologna in northern Italy. He never went. Instead, for the next twenty-four years, he lived 'undercover', but more or less openly, in Palermo.

15

The Mafia Turns Against the State: The Rise of Luciano Liggio

John Paul Getty III— Mafia kidnap victim

IN 1970, after a series of summit meetings in both Palermo and Milan—and after the heat from the police had lessened—the Sicilian Cupola was re-established, this time as a triumvirate, with Luciano Liggio representing the countryside families, and two bosses from Palermo—Gaetano Badalamenti and the young head of the Santa Maria del Jesù family, Stefano Bontate—the rest. Within a few months, though, something happened which was to show a new writing on the wall: the murder—by Liggio and Totò Riina, Buscetta later said—of the Palermo chief prosecutor, Pietro Scaglione.

Scaglione had, until that time at any rate, been at least a good friend of the Mafia's. He had 'lost' files

The Six Roses,
Sicily, 1971: key
crime figures held
under house arrest
by the Sicilian
authorities

and shelved cases, and made sure that Mafia defendants—including the entire family of Joe Bananas'
birthplace, Castellamare, arraigned for involvement
in the French Connection trade to the US—were
acquitted for lack of proof. It is possible that
Scaglione had changed his mind about helping the
Mafia and his death had been ordered by the
Commission. It is possible also that he was murdered on a personal basis by Liggio—as a *pentito*

(or turned Mafia witness) later said—for 'favouring Badalamenti' too much. But whatever the reason, it was an indication of how far certain members of Cosa Nostra were now prepared to go. No judge had been killed in Palermo since the War—it was an unwritten rule that they should remain untouched. A gauntlet had been thrown down which announced that no-one—not even the State—was invulnerable from now on.

If the murder was personal to Liggio, then it was also a significant slap in the face of the Commission—and this is the more likely explanation. Liggio—who was by now recovering from an operation for a bone disease (performed by the Italian President's personal surgeon in Rome)—was soon flouting its will in quite another way. His emissary in Palermo, Totò Riina, started kidnapping and holding for ransom members of rich local families. This cut right across the delicate ties the Mafia had established with both the hereditary landowners and the Christian Democrat establishment. It was a considerable embarrassment, but there was nothing the Commission could do, since both Badalamenti and Bontate were in Ucciardone Prison facing charges at the time. Only when they got out again was kidnapping finally and formally banned.

It must have been with some relief, then, that the Commission heard the news in 1972 that Liggio had left the island for Milan. It took him a while to return. On the mainland he took up kidnapping again, and had a hand in the snatching of John Paul Getty III, who famously lost part of an ear before his grandfather would pay the ransom. He was arrested and jailed in 1974, leaving the field open to his much more dangerous and subtle lieutenant, Totò Riina.

Totò Riina Begins to Take Power

Salvatore 'Totò'—or 'Shorty'—Riina was born in 1930, the son of a peasant family. He had little or no formal education. He only ever spoke limited Italian and hardly wrote at all. At the age of nineteen, though, he murdered a man—one of his own friends—and he was sent to prison. Out after six years—and by now a 'made' man—he quickly

attached himself to Luciano Liggio, who was deter-
minedly rising up through the ranks of the
Corleone family of Dr Navarra, the President of the
Cultivators' Association of Corleone and chairman
of the local branch of the Christian Democratic
Party. If Navarra had problems—with trade union
organizers, for example—Liggio always fixed them.
In the small, sprawling village of Corleone, there
were 153 murders in the years between 1953 and
1958.

However, both Liggio and his right hand Riina
were growing increasingly resentful of Navarra's
unwillingness to move with the times. This was a
point of view possibly put to them by Navarra's
cousin, a Sicilian-American called De Carlo, who
had fought in the War and had then settled, first in
Corleone, then in Palermo. In 1958 came a crisis:
while they were riding the two men were ambushed
by unknown assailants, though Navarra was suspected. Riina is said to have saved Liggio's life. After
they had killed Navarra their lives and careers
became more or less inseparable. Riina was given
preference over Liggio's other chief lieutenant,
Bernardo Provenzano, and though by now living on
the run, was sent to represent Liggio in Palermo.
Three years later, at about the same time Liggio went
to prison, he secretly married the sister of another
Corleonese soldier with whom he had four children.

One *pentito* witness later said of Riina: 'I never
saw him angry, sometimes a little flushed, but
never aggressive or rude.' Another remarked that he
had 'cunning and ferocity, a rare combination in
Cosa Nostra.' Tommaso Buscetta, the highest-rank-
ing witness of them all, said that, though he looked
like a peasant, he had a diplomatic manner 'and
God only knows how much diplomacy matters in
Cosa Nostra. He was a great persuader and he knew

how to work up people when he needed to.'

Buscetta also described him as living Cosa Nostra 'twenty-four hours a day. Always talking and discussing. Got information on everything. Followed every family's internal affairs. Got news from his spies. Cold and attentive to the smallest detail. . . he never tired of making suggestions, giving orders, handing out death sentences. . .'

Whether Liggio was pulling the strings from behind bars or not can't be known. But when the full six-man Commission was finally re-instituted in 1975 and reinforced the ban on kidnapping, the almost immediate reaction of Riina was to kidnap the father-in-law of Nino Salvo, one of the two cousins who had taken the Mafia into the tax-collection business and had made an extra fortune out of the money poured into Sicily after the earthquake in the Belice valley seven years before. The earthquake had killed 500 people and left 90,000 homeless; 60,000 people were still living in Nissen huts seven years later. Not a single new house had been built. The only things that the government's money seemed to have bought were roads that led nowhere and flyovers used by sheep. The roads and flyovers had been built by the Salvos.

The Salvos, then, were family—and the kidnap of the father-in-law was another severe embarrassment for the Palermitans on the Commission, particularly when he died of a heart attack before he could be returned. But then that was the point. Riina already had control over Palermo's mayor, the ex-barber from Corleone, Vito Ciancimino. Now he was announcing to the Commission and their pals that he was the only power—and as it turned out, the Commission had neither the will nor the necessary unity to resist him. Somehow he had Gaetano

Badalamenti thrown off the Commission—indeed expelled from the Mafia—and had his place taken by one of his own allies, Michele 'The Pope' Greco. After Badalamenti had fled to Brazil, Riina even managed to persuade the Commission that, as a man living under cover and thus with special needs, he should be assigned a couple of men from all of the other families to help him. He acquired, in other words, a small army of killers loyal only to him, who acted as both spies on, and bridges to, every one of his potential rivals.

By a mixture of fear and charm, Riina in the end came to hold them all in thrall. He divided and ruled them—and in the end he took them over completely.

16

The Montreal and Miami Connections

Montreal became
the staging post for
French Connection
heroin

THE MAIN DESTINATION for the heroin produced by the laboratories of the French Connection was Canada and the Mafia capital of Canada was Montreal. Montreal was close to the United States, it had a large Italian immigrant population, and being part of the French-speaking province of Quebec it was also a natural home-from-home for French and Corsican gangsters from Marseilles. It also had its own Mafia family, led by Vincent Cotroni, which was allied to the Bonanno family in New York.

Montreal, as a staging-post for French Connection heroin, seems to have been organized soon after the War by a man called Antoine d'Agostino, a French Corsican hood who may have been put in place by Lucky Luciano. He supplied the Genovese family and he was also one of the organizers of what came to be known—after another Luciano

Black Cadillacs
were the transport
of choice for the
Montreal smugglers

The Canadian
Royal Mounted
Police finally made
a breakthrough
against the drug
runners in 1961

protégé—as 'Gino's European Tours'. This involved
a steady flow of holidaying Italian families, travel-
ling by liner to Montreal—along with a car that had
been specially fitted out in either Italy or France.
From there they'd travel on—naturally enough—to
see the sights of New York, where the car would be
relieved of its hidden burden.

D'Agostino was run out of Canada in 1954, and
settled in Mexico, where he was to open a new
highway for heroin into the United States. The
Canada end of the business was at this point taken
over by Vincent Cotroni's younger brother,
Giuseppe 'Pep' Cotroni, and by Carmine Galante,
representing the New York Bonanno family. By
1956, these two—together with a representative of
the Genovese family—had control of some sixty
percent of the heroin then reaching the American
continent. It would be driven over the border in
Cadillacs with secret compartments that could only

Auguste Ricord set himself up in Buenos Aires and generated the South American connection

be opened if a number of the cars' gadgets were turned on at the same time. At its height, this seemingly foolproof method was delivering fifty kilos of refined heroin a month—with a street value of at least $50 million—into the United States.

The ring was broken open, though, in 1961 by a joint undercover operation of the US Bureau of Narcotics and the Canadian Royal Mounted Police. Pep Cotroni, Carmine Galante and the Genovese man were sent to jail. So another point of entry soon had to be found.

It was found in Miami, where Meyer Lansky was by now living in what seemed to be, on the surface at any rate, retirement. The boss of the city's Mafia was Santo Trafficante Jr., whose father had been a close associate both of Lansky's and Luciano's, and with Castro's revolution in Cuba, there were now any number of emigré Cuban couriers and hitmen—not to mention potential heroin addicts—available in the city. It also had access to traffic coming in from anywhere in the Caribbean, Central or South America. And these were the next staging posts from refined heroin arriving from Marseilles and Sicily—and elsewhere.

The Golden Triangle Comes On Line

By now both Turkey and the Lebanon were beginning to dry up as sources of morphine-base. But a new source was arriving on line—and once again through the good offices of America's cold-war warriors. As the French were forced to abandon their colonies in South-East Asia, the Americans arrived to take on communist insurgency in the region and soon became involved in roping in as allies the hill tribes of Laos—who happened to rely for survival on their opium crop. The price of their

Illegal immigrants went to work in New York's pizza parlours, bringing smuggled drugs with them—this became known as the Pizza Connection

involvement in the anti-communist struggle was the flying of their raw opium out onto the market by the CIA's proprietary airline, Air America. Once there, it was fed into a pipeline organized by the French-speaking Corsicans from Marseilles and their Sicilian allies, and processed into refined heroin both locally and in Europe. A good deal of the trade was financed by American-backed South Vietnamese generals and some of it by Santo Trafficante who made a tour of the area in 1962. Its most significant victims, ironically, were American GIs, who became hooked on heroin in alarming numbers.

With the Corsicans and their allies in Marseilles now in the game as major players, much of the new heroin was sent into the United States via a South American network that had been set up after the War by a Marseilles hood called Auguste Ricord. Basing himself in Buenos Aires and Asuncion, Paraguay— where protection from the unimaginably venal régime was simply a matter of money—Ricord had organized a group of pilots, couriers and strong-arms who used various methods to run contraband into North America—via carrier 'mules' or else by plane to Mexico, from where it would be either driven over the border or else flown to Miami by light air-craft. In the ten years up to his arrest in 1971, Ricord's group, which was joined by fugitives from Marseilles, is reckoned to have moved five tonnes of ninety percent pure heroin into North America, worth at least $1 billion.

A favourite port of entry for the heroin arriving

President Nixon's war on drugs was a constant thorn in the Mafia's money-making plans

both from Europe and the Far East was Buenos Aires, which had a large Italian population—as did Sao Paolo in Brazil, which was where many of the Sicilian Mafia, exiled as a result of the island's gang wars, settled. But it was not by any means the only one. Some of the heroin went directly to Mexico, where it was shifted, first by what was left of Antoine d'Agostino's Corsican network, and then by a group financed by a wealthy businessman, Jorge Asaf y Bala, known as 'the Al Capone of Mexico'.

Another favourite gateway remained Montreal, though the method of shifting the heroin over the border had necessarily changed. Now it was carried over by illegal immigrants, most of them Sicilian, who went to work in the pizza restaurants controlled by the Mafia, particularly in New York City. Over time these pizza joints became the main storage and distribution points for imported heroin—the so-called Pizza Connection. The Sicilians were used as expert and untraceable hit-men by the local families, particularly by the Bonnano family which was riven by internal fighting over the heroin-spoils.

The Price of Riches

The spoils, it has to be emphasized, were enormous. One small-time Sicilian boss, later turned *pentito*, said of them: 'We all became millionaires. Suddenly, within a couple of years. Thanks to

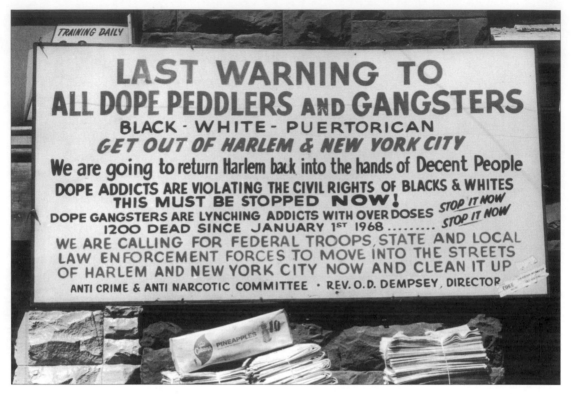

Local communities
finally took the law
into their own
hands in the war
against drugs

drugs.' Money poured into the island. Between 1970 and 1980, the turnover of banks in Sicily increased fourfold—and the number of banks, immune from inspection by the central authorities, multiplied hugely. The little town of Trapani, for example, with a population of 70,000, at one point had more banks than did the whole city of Milan, Italy's financial hub.

The money made everything possible. More and more of the heroin-refining labs were moved to Sicily, as President Nixon's war on drugs finally persuaded the French authorities to move against the Marseilles French Connection. But the money was also divisive. More than ever before it allowed individual Mafiosi to become entrepreneurs in their own right, financing and profiting from the trade in all kinds of different ways. This was destabilizing to the old order. It cut across established ties, like the ties that bound Joe Bananas to his drug-running relatives in Castellamare and those that yoked Carlo Gambino's family to that of his cousins in Palermo, Salvatore Inzerillo and Rosario Spatola.

It also meant that the stakes, both to risk and to play for, had become very much higher. It was true that the judiciary and police had extremely limited powers of investigation. They were not allowed access, for example, to the records of individual bank accounts, which were private and privileged, however suspect. But there were other ways of coming close: tracing international bank transfers, for example, or tracking down the hidden laboratories. And there was also by now a further added complication: one caused by the bank-collapse of the Mafia's chief financier Michele Sindona.

The Mafia's Banker

Michele Sindona: the Sicilian Mafia's bank manager

Michele Sindona was born in Patti, a town on the north coast of Sicily. His father dealt in funerary wreaths, but son Michele—after an early meeting, it is said, with Vito Genovese—came to specialize in banks. By 1961, he was the majority partner in the Banca Privata Finanzaria in Milan, and it was almost certainly then—when the massive profits from heroin were on the horizon—that he became the Sicilian Mafia's bank manager.

He also, though, served several other major interests along his way to the top. He was, for example, the conduit for the CIA money that poured first into Greece at the time of the colonels' coup of 1968, and then arrived, four years later—$11 million of it—in the campaign funds of anti-communist Italian politicians. He had extremely close ties to the Christian Democratic

Party and in 1969, via his purchase of the Vatican's property development company, he became financial advisor to Pope Paul VI. By now he controlled five banks and well over 100 companies in eleven countries. Yet this same Sindona had been identified two years earlier, in a 1967 letter sent by the head of Interpol in Washington to the Italian police, as being heavily involved in drug trafficking.

Nothing at all happened. By now Sindona was regarded by the world's financial press as the most successful businessman in Italy and in 1971 he aimed right for the pinnacle, for control over the two biggest holding companies in Italy. With the first, he was successful. He took over the board and installed his own people, among them an obscure banker who was later to become extremely famous, Roberto Calvi. But the second takeover was blocked by the Bank of Italy, which ordered an inspection of Sindona's bank holdings.

Massive illegalities were found, but the Bank of Italy did nothing. By this time Sindona had taken over the eighteenth largest bank in the United States, the Franklin National, and had moved to New York. There he secretly speculated against the lira, only to be called in by the Italian government to repair the damage he'd done. Little by little, though, he was losing his touch. He lost a vast amount of money on the markets, and by October 1974 the game was up. Within a few days of each other, his banks on both sides of the Atlantic collapsed. Days before the Franklin National caved in, the Federal Reserve Bank had lent Sindona $1.7 billion to save it.

It was the largest bank collapse in the history of both the United States and Italy. It cost Italy the rough modern equivalent of $5.5 billion. It also cost the Vatican a huge unknown amount, and the

Sicilian Cosa Nostra a great deal more, perhaps several billion dollars of the drug money that was by now pouring in from the American market. The Cosa Nostra also had two extra problems: Sindona himself (now living at the Pierre Hotel in New York on bail of $3 million), and a particularly dogged and stubborn man who had been appointed as receiver to investigate Sindona's banks in Milan: Giorgio Ambrosoli.

Considerable efforts were made with senior figures in the Christian Democratic Party to get Sindona off the hook even now. Sindona knew where the bodies were buried, and exactly how high in the Party Cosa Nostra's tentacles reached, as we shall see. But receiver Ambrosoli was not to be shaken off. He soon found Sindona's secret mother-company in Liechtenstein and a web of other companies within companies stretching away from it across the world. It was clear he had to be silenced—and in early July 1979, he was: shot down in front of his house in Milan by an unknown assailant.

That left Sindona himself—and three weeks after Ambrosoli's assassination, he simply disappeared from the Pierre Hotel in New York. His secretary received a message saying that he'd been kidnapped by 'communist terrorist kidnappers'. But in fact, under the wing of Carlo Gambino's son, he was taken to Palermo for meetings with Cosa Nostra's high command. It was from there that there now issued a number of messages from the 'kidnappers', threatening to extort from Sindona full details of Italy's capital exporters and their foreign bank accounts, the companies which had been used to bribe politicians, and so on. It was a threat to bring down the whole Italian economic and political establishment and a meeting in Vienna was set with those concerned 'to arrange for Sindona's release'.

In the end, a letter carrying instructions to Sindona's lawyer about the Vienna meeting was intercepted as the result of a telephone-tap. It was being carried by a Mafia courier, the brother of Rosario Spatola. So the meeting in Vienna was called off, and Sindona was soon back in the Pierre Hotel once more, announcing that he'd been released by his 'kidnappers'.

In the end, after legal manoeuvrings on both sides of the Atlantic, Sindona received prison terms for fraud, and in 1986 a life sentence in Italy for the murder of Ambrosoli. He never, though, gave up any of his extraordinary secrets. Still, three days after the Ambrosoli judgment, in the maximum-security prison at Vighera, where he was supposed to be watched twenty-four hours a day, Sindona died—like Lucky Luciano—after drinking a cup of coffee.

17

The Second Sicilian Mafia War

T HIS, THEN, was the situation in Palermo in the summer of 1979: Michele Sindona was holed up in a villa belonging to Italian-American doctor and freemason Joseph Miceli Crimi. He was trying to blackmail, under Cosa Nostra direction, the Italian establishment, including Prime Minister Giulio Andreotti, to rescue his banks and reimburse the Mafia's money. The Commission was smarting under the loss of a huge pile of its profits and it was beginning to have a sense that, for the first time, it was not being properly protected by the Christian Democrats. The police and investigating magistrates were now getting too close; the old order was dying and Liggio and Riina were threatening takeover.

It was then that the killings began in earnest. Already Michele Reina, the provincial secretary of the Christian Democrats for Palermo, had been gunned down to get the attention of his political bosses in Rome. Then in late July, Boris Giuliano, the deputy police chief, was assassinated—he'd had a suspiciously long meeting with Ambrosoli in Milan three days before the receiver had been killed. Next was Cesare Terranova, a crusading judge who'd just taken over as chief examining magistrate in Palermo and had vowed to nail Luciano Liggio as Public Enemy Number One: he was gunned down just 100 yards from his apartment along with his police bodyguard Lenin Mancuso.

This was not the end of the list of what came to be known as 'illustrious corpses'. On 6 January 1980, Piersanti Mattarella, the Christian Democrat president of the Sicilian region, was killed for standing in Cosa Nostra's way. And within a matter of months there were two more deaths. First was Emanuele Basile, the captain of the *carabinieri* who'd taken over from Giuliano the investigation of the Mafia's finances. He was shot repeatedly in the back whilst carrying his four-year-old daughter, who was miraculously unhurt. Then the chief prosecutor of Palermo, Gaetano Costa, was calmly assassinated while browsing at a bookstall near his home.

These killings, coming so quickly together, were unprecedented. They seem to have led to a final split in the Commission, which was by now packed with allies of Riina and Liggio. The last two independent chieftains on it were increasingly isolated, and though an attempt at reconciliation was made by the respected Mafioso Tommaso Buscetta, it was unsuccessful—and, while on day release from prison, Buscetta fled to Brazil. It was just as well. In April 1981, his friend Stefano Bontate was gunned down on his forty-second birthday while stopped at a traffic light in his Alfa Romeo. Salvatore Inzerillo soon followed him, murdered just as he was about to step into a new bullet-proof car after leaving his mistress' house. The same gun, an AK47, was used in both assassinations.

What followed was a massacre. In 1981 and 1982, there were at least 200 bodies on the streets of Palermo, besides 300 more disappearances—victims of the *lupara biancha*, the 'white shotgun'. One entire Mafia family was wiped out while guests at lunches hosted by Riina and Michael 'The Pope' Greco on a single afternoon. The soldiers of Inzerillo and Bontate—even their relatives—were tracked down and killed. Inzerillo's sixteen-year-old son, who'd threatened to kill Riina, had his right, shooting arm cut off before he was murdered, his uncle disappeared from his house in New Jersey, and his brother was found in the trunk of a car in New York with his genitals cut off and with dollars stuffed into the mouth of his severed head. Gaetano Badalamenti's nephew—who'd taken over his family after his expulsion—was also assassinated. And not even the mediator Tommaso Buscetta was immune. His two sons, his son-in-law, his brother, his nephew—even the brother of his first wife—either disappeared or joined the list of those shot down.

There were also two more 'illustrious' corpses' in 1982—and these were the most shocking of all. One was Pio La Torre, a communist member of parliament from Sicily who'd recently proposed a swingeing anti-Mafia law. It was designed to make membership of Cosa Nostra a serious crime, to permit access to all banking records when such a crime was being investigated, and to allow the government to seize all assets suspected of ammassment by crime. That was bad enough. But the second corpse soon had all Italy bearing down on Sicily. He was a national hero: General Carlo Alberto Dalla Chiesa, the newly appointed Prefect for Palermo.

The Assassination of General Alberto Dalla Chiesa

General Dalla Chiesa knew Sicily well. Early in his career he had been stationed in Corleone during the days of Dr Navarra. Later, in the Sixties and early Seventies, he had done another tour of duty as commander of the *carabinieri* in Palermo. But he'd since achieved national fame by breaking the back of the well-organized terrorist Red Brigades which had paralysed the country. Now he was expected to do the same for the Sicilian Mafia.

His first official duty was to attend the funeral of La Torre—where workers and young people gathered outside, chanting slogans like 'Lima. . .! Ciancimino! Chi di voi è l'assassino?' (Which of you is the assassin?) and 'Governo DC, La Mafia sta lì!' (The Mafia was there, inside the Democratic Christian government!). But he was outfoxed from the start. He demanded special powers from the government, but they never materialized. He became increasingly isolated. Using tax records, property deeds and rental records, he did begin to follow a thread of clues deep into the relationship between business, politics and the Mafia—and also into the alliance between the Corleonesi and the families of Catania on the other side of the island. But he never got far. Four months after his arrival, he and his young wife were on their way to a restaurant with his bodyguard when their car was surrounded by gunmen on motorbikes, who forced them off the road and killed them. The assassins included Giuseppe Greco and 21-year-old Giuseppe Lucchese. It was later said that there had been Mafia surveillance-teams all over Palermo that evening, using two-way radios to monitor the Dalla Chiesas' whereabouts.

So perhaps his enemies knew that on the very

General Dalla Chiesa broke the back of the Red Brigades and was expected to do the same with the Mafia last day of his life he'd paid a secret visit to the American consul in Palermo, asking him to urge the American government to put pressure on the Italians to give him both the powers he needed and the passing of the proposed La Torre law. He seemed to know that he was being deliberately denied them. In a newspaper interview before Dalla Chiesa's death, he'd said:

'I have clear ideas about what needs to be done... [and] I have already illustrated these ideas to the competent authorities [some time ago]. I hope there will be some very rapid response. If not, we cannot hope for positive results.' He went on, in what sounds like weariness and resignation: 'I believe I have understood the new rules of the game: the powerful government servant gets killed when two conditions intertwine: he has both become too dangerous and at the same time he is isolated and therefore killable.'

Tommaso Buscetta, at the time in Brazil, later said of Dalla Chiesa's death: 'General Dalla Chiesa had to be killed because he was in possession of secrets.' Salvo Lima, the Mafia's representative in government, apparently agreed. He's reported as having said after the La Torre law was finally passed after Dalla Chiesa's death: 'For certain Romans he was more dangerous shoved aside with a pension than as Prefect with special powers.' Why?

The Mafia Goes into National Politics

To answer this question, we have to go back to the aftermath of the War and to the founding of the American- (and Pope-) backed Christian Democratic Party. Since 1947 the Christian Democrats had never been out of government—and were in fact to remain in power until 1992. Throughout this whole period Sicily—after the first election, at any rate—was a Christian Democratic stronghold; the votes—which represented ten per-cent of the whole Italian electorate—were regularly and reliably delivered by the Mafia. When the Mafia itself successfully got into politics, then, and took over the machinery of the local Party, it was only natural that it should go looking for a sponsor and patron at the highest level. Its choice soon fell on the wiliest Christian Democrat of them all, Giulio Andreotti.

When Salvo Lima, the former mayor of Palermo, became a member of parliament in 1968, he soon made approaches to Andreotti, whose support, he believed, was too narrowly based in the area in and around Rome. Lima at the time belonged to another faction of the Christian Democrats, but, as a close associate of Andreotti's later recalled: 'I met Lima.. . and he said to me: 'If I switch over to Andreotti, I'm not going to come alone, but with my lieu-tenants, colonels, infantry, fanfares and flags.' We talked for three days non-stop, and when the day arrived for the meeting in Andreotti's office. . . Lima really *did* come as the head of an army.'

As a reward for his support, Lima was made under-secretary at the Ministry of Finance during Andreotti's second term as prime minister, and was actually made Minister of the Budget in 1974. However, a leading economist at the Ministry resigned, having read about Lima's record as Mayor of Palermo, and eleven requests to impeach Lima soon reached parliament. Though none of them were acted on, Lima, in the end, had to be sidelined as a European MP.

The Death and Documents of Aldo Moro

By that time, though, as it later transpired, Andreotti had had meetings in Sicily, not only with the entire local Christian Democratic apparatus, but also with the Commission. He was, so to speak, a part of the family—and one very important man knew it: the president of the Christian Democratic party Aldo Moro.

Aldo Moro was the prime minister who in the 1970s forged a 'historic compromise' with the Italian Communist Party, who commanded one-third of the vote, that was designed to change the face of Italian politics forever. On the morning of March 16, 1978, he was on his way to the swearing-in of the government of his successor as prime minister, Giulio Andreotti, who would govern for the first time with communist backing. He never arrived. His car was ambushed by members of the left-wing terrorist Red Brigades, his bodyguards and driver were killed and he was kidnapped. They would return him, they said, if the founder members of the Red Brigades, then in jail, were released.

In the meantime, he was 'interrogated' and 'tried' and—according to the communiqués issued by his captors—had written a series of letters to his friends among the Christian Democrats, begging them to negotiate his release. They'd refused. The government said it was not 'in the national interest' to negotiate with *terroristi*. Besides, it was clear that the letters—which grew increasingly bitter— were either 'written under duress' or actually 'dictated by' the terrorists. Why they refused to negotiate wasn't clear to many people, since they'd negotiated over hostages with the Red Brigades before. But they remained obdurate—with the honorable exceptance of the socialists in

President of the
Christian
Democratic party,
Aldo Moro

parliament—and Moro was in effect condemned to death. A member of the Sicilian Commission, Pippo Calò, their representative in Rome at the time, explained why, according to a later *pentito*. 'You don't understand,' he'd said when Stefano Bontate had suggested that Cosa Nostra should mount a rescue mission, 'Leaders in his own party don't want him free.' Just under eight weeks after he had been abducted his dead body was found in the trunk of a car on the Via Caetani in the centre of Rome.

Less than five months later, anti-terrorist police under General Dalla Chiesa raided an apartment in Milan and arrested nine members of the Red Brigades who were busily typing out copies of letters and notes that Moro hadn't sent and a transcript of his long interrogation. The documents subsequently disappeared, and only an edited version was ever released—and this seemed to do nothing more than reheat old gossip about Andreotti. But it was soon clear that two people at least had seen the full version: first, Mino Pecorelli, the editor of a muck-raking journal, *Osservatore Politico*, and secondly General Dalla Chiesa—and the two of them seem to have had regular meetings. Pecorelli was shot dead in the street in March 1979 before he could publish it. But by then, so it later transpired,

Dalla Chiesa had given a copy to Andreotti and asked for his comments.

What was in these documents, no-one at the time knew. Andreotti claimed later never to have read them. But twelve years later, in 1990, workmen renovating that very same Milan apartment found hidden behind a plaster panel what seemed to be another complete copy of the Red Brigades' Moro documents, and they were very damning indeed. They announced that a secret anti-communist military network had been set up at the end of the War with the help of the Americans—and was still in existence, that the Christian Democratic Party was funded by the CIA and that the Italian state had been involved in fomenting right-wing terrorism in the Seventies. They also provided evidence of an extremely close relationship between Andreotti and Michele Sindona, and claimed to have proof that Andreotti had used a nationally-owned bank to make loans to his cronies, some of them involving money from Mafia launderers run by the Commission's representative in Rome, Pippo Calò.

If they had been revealed at the time, they would have destroyed Andreotti's career. As it was, they were probably responsible for the death of General Dalla Chiesa. Palermo, after all, was a much more dangerous place than Rome—especially for an isolated man with little real power, and one, moreover, already being whispered against.

18

Sam Giancana, the Mafia and the Death of JFK

Were the Mafia involved in American spon sored attempts to assassinate Castro?

I N THE UNITED STATES, the Mafia, perhaps, has never aimed quite so high. But it should be remembered that in the 1960 election, which brought President John Kennedy into office, the outcome in the end was decided by a few hundred thousand votes and that the Democratic majority in Cook County, Illinois was finally key.

Cook County, Illinois just happens to have been Al Capone's old stamping-ground, as Kennedy's father Joe, who'd been a bootlegger and had associated with the Italian Mafia, knew well; and Mafia boss Sam Giancana—who shared at least one lover with President Kennedy—later boasted of having swung the election there for Joe's son as a favour. Giancana and the Mafia were also involved in American-sponsored attempts to kill Fidel Castro of Cuba and several of the conspiracy theories surrounding the assassination of

John Kennedy's possible links with the Mafia have long been the subject of whispered discussion

the President in November 1963 claim that he was killed at the behest of the American Mafia because he refused to return the favour it had done him. Indeed, by allowing his brother, Attorney-General Robert Kennedy, to investigate organized crime and Teamsters Union boss Jimmy Hoffa, he'd made matters much worse.

We will probably never know the truth of any of this. But then that's in the nature of our knowledge of the Cosa Nostra. It exists in the shadows, and only very occasionally does it come out into the light, through the confessions of *pentiti*, via wiretaps, at

Sam Giancana, who
shared at least one
lover with
President Kennedy

Jimmy Hoffa and
the Teamsters
Union came under
intense scrutiny
from Attorney
General Robert
Kennedy

trials. The rest is silence, discretion. As Tommaso Buscetta, the most famous and highest-ranked of all the *pentiti*, said: 'In my ambience no-one asks direct questions, but your interlocutor, when he considers it necessary, makes you understand, with a nod of the head, with a smile. . . even simply by his silence.'

Added to this is the fact that the family bosses and the members of the New York and Sicilian Commissions are far, far removed from the actual commitment of any crime. They live at the top of a pyramid: outwardly respectable businessmen—sometimes, it is true, with no visible source of income, but sometimes with an income that, on the surface at any rate, seems quite legitimate. Salvatore Inzerillo's brother-in-law Rosario Spatola in Sicily, for example, had made millions of dollars from construction alone. He was said to be the fifth-highest payer of taxes in the whole of Italy.

Silence, remoteness, wisdom, power: these, then, were—and are—the watchwords that govern the behaviour of the senior ranks of Cosa Nostra. They were—and are—the law: a law that was regularly broken, however, by the head of one of New York's five families: Joe Bananas.

Joe Bananas and the Heroin Business

Joe Bananas: by all accounts 'a flake'

Joe Bananas—or Giuseppe Bonanno—was, by the consensus of the other members of the Commission and even his own street-soldiers, a flake. Quite apart from his heroin business, of which many of the bosses still disapproved, he was, in the early Sixties, trying to take over territory on the West Coast: he was treading on other bosses' toes. There were even rumours that he was plotting against other Commission members.

As if this wasn't bad enough, in 1964, he made his own son Bill his family's *consigliere*, thus flying in the face of Mafia tradition. More senior people had been passed over, and in any case Bill Bonanno had been born with a silver spoon in his mouth: he couldn't even talk the language of the streets. An internal civil war broke out. Complaints were made to the Commission, and the boss of a minor New Jersey family called Sam 'The Plumber' Cavalcante was appointed, either to bring the family back together or—and this may have been the Commission's intention—to split it further apart.

As it happened, the FBI had a wiretap in Sam The Plumber's office and were able to listen in when he had a meeting with one of his captains, who was also the business agent for a New Jersey-based union. From the conversation between the two men, the FBI found out that both Bill Bonanno and father Joe were refusing to answer summonses

Jack Ruby killed
Lee Harvey Oswald
—was it on Mafia
orders?

from the Commission. 'When Joe defies the Commission, he's defying the whole world!' exclaimed the outraged Cavalcante.

Why Joe Bananas wasn't killed remains a mystery. In October 1964 he was kidnapped by armed men off the streets of Manhattan only to reappear two years later, looking fit and well, at a courthouse in Manhattan's Foley Square. He gave himself up to a judge, but wouldn't explain where he'd been and faced a minor charge for obstruction of justice. At this point he retired to a house in Tucson, Arizona, as if nothing had happened.

Whether he continued to run his family from Tucson is unknown. What is known is that the Bonannos' New York territory, including the heroin business, was little by little eaten away in the late Sixties and early Seventies by the family of Carlo Gambino and that in 1973 Phil 'Rusty' Rastelli was elected head of the Bonnanos, though perhaps denied a seat on the Commission. The inference is that Rastelli was weak—and this put both him and the Gambinos at odds with the murderous ex-*consigliere* of the Bonanno family, Carmine Galante.

Carmine Galante

Carmine Galante's Mafia nickname was 'Lilo'—for the little cigars he constantly smoked. He was short, fat, bald and immensely violent. When he came out of federal prison in 1978 he had two ambitions: to make money by taking back control of the immensely lucrative New York heroin trade and to become the ultimate man of respect: the *capo di tutti capi.*

Galante grew up in East Harlem, New York, the son of Sicilian immigrants. He was to remain a Sicilian, out of tune with the pliable Italo-American businessmen who gradually took over the Mafia. He

Carmine Galante
was a man of
vendettas

was another Riina, a man of vendettas; he lived by the gun and the code of honour and as such he became in the early days a highly-trusted member of the Bonanno family.

In the mid-Fifties, as we have seen, he organized the so-called Montreal Connection and in 1957 travelled as *consigliere* to Joe Bananas to the Palermo summit of Sicilian and American Mafia leaders organized by Luciano. In 1962, he was sentenced to twenty years for his part in the Montreal Connection and by the time he was released on parole in 1974 he had had plenty of time to consider his response to the new order he faced.

His timing was opportune. Carlo Gambino, whom he

Galante shuns the spotlight with the help of some associates

loathed for the inroads he'd made into Bonanno turf, was ill and soon died, and his family was taken over by his brother-in-law Paul 'Big Paulie' Castellano. Phil Rastelli was behind bars at the time—and he rapidly stood down as soon as Galante hit the streets. Galante had also planned well, for he'd gathered around himself a large group of old-country Sicilian hit-men who had no allegiance to anyone but himself—and to the Mafia code he believed in. They quickly muscled and killed their way back to control of the heroin business.

Galante, then, rapidly became a 'business problem' to the Commission, especially to 'Big Paulie'. But no-one seems to have wanted a bullying throwback, a 'Moustache Pete' from the past, to rock the boat. So the Commission ordered Galante's assassi-

Galante grew up on
the tough streets of
East Harlem

nation—and the job was handed, as per custom, to a member of his own family, underboss Salvatore Catalano.

On July 13, 1979, as Galante was enjoying an after-dinner cigar with two friends on the patio of Joe and Mary's Italian Restaurant in Brooklyn, three men wearing ski-masks and shotguns walked in through the back door. Galante was dead so fast, his cigar was still in his mouth as he hit the patio floor. The traditional .45 bullet was then fired into his left eye and his guests were finished off by his own trusted bodyguards who then calmly walked out with his killers.

That same day, at a meeting in prison, Phil Rastelli was reconfirmed as head of the Bonanno family, and Mafia bosses met in a social club in New York's Little Italy to celebrate. But Galante later came back to haunt them. As the result of wiretaps installed during the investigation into the so-called Pizza Connection, Salvatore Catalano and the members of the New York Commission were eventually charged with plotting his murder, though Bonanno foot soldier Anthony 'Bruno' Indelicato was convicted of actually pulling the trigger.

19

The Pizza Connection

THE PIZZA CONNECTION as far as American law enforcement was concerned began in 1971, when US customs agents at New York's docks discovered eighty-two kilos of ninety-percent pure heroin hidden in a car brought in by an Italian cruise liner. They arrested the Gambino man who eventually took delivery—and 'he turned out to run a pizza-joint. In fact all the evidence thrown up by the case seemed to have some connection with pizzas and with a pizzeria-operator called Michael Piancone. The arrested man ran a Piancone Pizza Palace and two brothers, Salvatore and Matteo Sollena, who were both suspected of some involvement, ran several.

The investigation at the time didn't get very far. But then in 1978 it came alive again. Salvatore Sollena's girlfriend was picked up by New Jersey police for carrying counterfeit money, and was found to be in possession of some real money as well: $51,000 in cash, in fact, and $25,000 in cashier's cheques. It transpired that she and the Sollena brothers had earlier bought a further

$330,000-worth of cashier's cheques, all in values of under $10,000, which meant it didn't have to be reported by the bank. These had then been transferred to an account in Palermo.

A year later, US customs found out that a further $4 million had been shipped over the past two years from New Jersey to Palermo, $1 million of it by a small-time pizza operator in New York. And in June of that year, Boris Giuliano, the Palermo police chief who was to be killed shortly afterwards, found $497,000 in cash in a suitcase at Palermo airport. It had been wrapped in pizza aprons that were traced to a pizzeria owned by Salvatore Sollena in New Jersey.

At the beginning of 1980, the Drug Enforcement Agency (DEA), the FBI and the US Customs service decided to come together in a joint operation, and they soon discovered that most of the targets they were led to were Sicilian. They were also working under the aegis of the two families with the closest connections to Sicily, the Bonannos and Gambinos. The man in charge seemed to be another Sicilian immigrant, Salvatore Catalano, who had organized the killing of Carmine Galante and who owned a bakery and a half-interest in a pizzeria in Queens.

In the autumn of that year, a fancy Mafia wedding was held at the affluent Hotel Pierre in New York, and both Salvatore Catalano and his partner in pizza, Giuseppe Ganci, were guests, alongside major figures in the Sicilian, Canadian and American Mafias: among them relatives of the late Carlo Gambino, Salvatore Inzerillo from the Sicilian Commission, and money-launderers and financial advisers from Montreal, Sicily and Milan. The watching joint task-force made a record of the numbers they called during the reception, and the owners of these numbers were then traced and watched. With the net spreading, the task-force finally applied for permission to use wire-taps.

Moving forward was at first a slow affair. But then in 1983, the task-force had a lucky break. In two separate sting operations in Philadelphia, undercover DEA agents made offers to buy heroin from two suspected dealers, one a pizzeria owner—and both of them immediately called Ganci's Al Dente pizzeria in Queens, the one he owned with Catalano. Both dealers were then watched as they made the buys (for over $350,000). By following Ganci's movements, as well as his telephone calls, the team were able to start making a list of his associates, who were also then tapped.

It was long and difficult work. Not only did the members of the Pizza Connection talk in Sicilian dialect, they also used public pay phones rather than the phones of their restaurants and homes—and they changed phones and talked all the time. As a result the problems of both wiretapping and transcription of conversations rapidly mushroomed. Help, though, was soon at hand. For in another part of the investigation, the team was following the trail of the heroin money, and that soon came up trumps.

Where the Money Goes

Phones were a problem for the Pizza Connection, but so was the money: huge amounts of it, mostly in small bills paid over by street-corner addicts. At first this had not been too much of a problem—the money would simply be picked up in suitcases and flown to Switzerland. But then the Connection had to start using a special—and highly athletic—money-changer, whose job it was to pick up the cash each week and run it from bank to bank in

New York, turning it along the way into cashier's cheques, all of them for under $10,000. Soon even that wasn't enough. So the money-changer took to hiring private planes and freighting the money, millions of dollars at a time, to a discreet private bank in the off-shore tax haven of Bermuda, from where it could be passed on to Swizerland.

This worked well for a while, but then the volume of money increased even more and special squads of Swiss couriers had to be brought in— their job simply to pick up as much money as they could and fly it straight back to Switzerland. The problem now, though, was that with so many people involved there were inevitably thefts. So in the end the Connection took the path the Mafia were to take forever on into the future: they turned to the major financial institutions.

Over a period of less than six months in 1982, a Swiss financier called Franco Della Torre deposited at least $20 million in accounts at Merrill Lynch and E. F. Hutton in New York's financial district. The money was then passed through finance companies he'd set up in and around Lugano and then laundered by being moved through yet more accounts till it reached its destination: either in a Swiss bank or in the account of a Mafia-fronted enterprise in Italy. Investigators believe that in the six years the part of the Pizza Connection they were watching operated, $1.6 billion of profit was cleaned in this and other ways.

The main heroin suppliers to the Connection were Peppino Soresi in Sicily, known as 'the doctor from far away', and Gaetano Badalamenti: the same Gaetano Badalamenti who'd been expelled from both the Commission and the Mafia in Sicily and whose nephew had later been killed by Riina. Badalamenti was now operating from Brazil, and he was in regular contact with the Connection, either through a nephew who lived in Illinois or directly via the pay-phones. It was via the pay-phones in October 1983 that the surveillance team learned that the Connection was in need of large deliveries from one or both of their suppliers at the beginning of 1984. But there were delays, prevarications and arguments about terms of payment and delivery. Soon the tempers in New York, Brazil and Sicily were getting fraught. Finally, Badalamenti demanded a crash meeting with his nephew in Madrid: FBI and DEA agents, deciding this was much too good an opportunity to miss, went along.

Badalamenti was arrested in Madrid on April 8, 1984. The next morning, with coordinated arrests in Italy, Switzerland and the United States, the Pizza Connection was closed down.

20

Giovanni Falcone and Tommaso Buscetta, The Don of Two Worlds

Prosecuting magistrate Giovanni Falcone

O N THE DAY of Badalamenti's arrest, Tommaso Buscetta was in jail in Brazil, facing extradition to Italy and a meeting with Palermo prosecuting magistrate Giovanni Falcone. He wasn't to know it at the time, but in a sense he and Falcone were two of a kind. Falcone was not only a native Palermitan, but also one of the most knowledgeable men on earth about the workings of the Sicilian Mafia. From almost the first days of his appointment he'd been drawn into the Mafia's webs, because that was where all his cases seemed to lead him. And he'd been encouraged in this by his boss and close friend, Rocco Chinnici, the successor as chief prosecutor of the murdered Cesare Terranova.

He'd looked into the heroin traffic between south-east Asia and Sicily after 233 kilos of refined heroin had been found on a ship in the Suez Canal. He'd even taken on the tax-collector millionaires, Nino and Ignazio Salvo. He'd had the financial police search their Palermo offices and homes and remove thirty cartons of documents, and he'd found out some interesting things: that ninety-seven per cent of the money the cousins had spent on their opulent Zagarella Hotel in Palermo, for example, had been paid for by the Italian government and that the hotel was not only a favourite for Mafia celebrations but also for those of the ruling Christian Democrats. A wedding party given by a Sicilian parliamentarian for 1800 guests hadn't cost him a single *lira*.

He'd also signed with Chinnici the warrant for the arrest, for the murder of General Dalla Chiesa, of Totò Riina and the members of the Palermo Cupola. And then, three weeks later, in July 1983, he'd had to attend the funeral of what was left of his friend Chinnici, killed by a car-bomb along with his driver, two bodyguards and the doorman of his apartment building. Michele Greco was later sentenced to life imprisonment for Chinnici's assassination.

Falcone was a serious man; so was Buscetta. When they finally met in the Rebibia prison in Rome they must have both recognized as much. Buscetta began talking, and went on talking for almost two months—and what he said was to shake the Mafia on both sides of the Atlantic to its very foundations.

Buscetta: 'Reviving the Mafia's Honour'

Tommaso Buscetta in court

Tommaso Buscetta was born in Palermo in July 1928, the son of a glass-maker. He left school at fourteen, and a year later he came to the attention of the Mafia—or Cosa Nostra ('Our Thing'), as he called it, identifying its real name for the very first time—when he killed a number of German soldiers. This was enough to qualify him for entry into 'the Honoured Society'. He was inducted into the Porta Nuova family by its boss, Gaetano Filippone, at the age of eighteen.

For a while he worked in the family glass-making business. He got married to a pregnant girlfriend but couldn't seem to settle down. He worked for a time in Turin and even briefly became a trade-union activist back in Palermo. Finally, in 1948, he emigrated to Argentina with his wife and two children. He set up glass factories, first in Buenos Aires and then in Sao Paolo, Brazil. But his wife couldn't settle. So in 1951—reluctantly—he returned to Sicily.

Buscetta spoke wistfully to Falcone about the old traditions of Cosa Nostra and the 'men of respect' he encountered when he returned. He clearly regarded the new breed of Mafiosi—those who'd killed seven members of his family, including two of his sons—as betrayers of a long and honorable tradition. And he began for Falcone the long story of his life, beginning with his first meetings with Lucky Luciano in the early Fifties, the Palermo summit with Joe Bananas in 1957 and Liggio's killing of Dr Navarra, which he said was the beginning of the end of the old traditions. He talked about the setting up of the Commission, in which he'd played a major role and about the first Mafia Wars of the 1960s, which he'd fled, first for Mexico and then the United States.

About his own connection to crimes, Buscetta was uncharacteristically reticent. But it was plain from the first to Falcone—as Buscetta laid out everything: the structures of Cosa Nostra, the make-up of the Commissions, the names of those involved in the drugs trade—that he'd been a man of great influence. He'd probably been involved in the early stages of the Pizza Connection; he'd almost certainly had a hand in the takeover by the Sicilians of the Corsican networks in Latin America; and he may even have been responsible, along with Michele Zaza of Naples' so-called 'New' Family, for the coordination of cocaine-exports to Europe and the United States. But Falcone didn't care in the end. Buscetta was known as the 'Don of Two Worlds', the most important Mafia witness ever to confess voluntarily—and what he was saying was gold dust.

About half-way through their sessions, Falcone called in his American counterpart, who had become close to Buscetta's third wife. Together they began to talk about the possibility of Buscetta giving evidence on both sides of the Atlantic. He quietly agreed. He didn't want any special consideration for himself, he said, but he would be glad if help could be given to his family. He quite clearly believed that what he was doing was for the compromised honour of the old days and ways, the old Cosa Nostra.

21

Mass Arrests in Sicily and New York

O
N THE BASIS OF BUSCETTA'S
testimony and what Falcone and his
fellow members of the Sicilian Anti-
Mafia Pool already knew, Operation
San Michele was launched in the early morning of
September 29, 1984. Armed with more than 350
warrants, police closed off the streets of Palermo
and began their arrests, pulling Mafia leaders and
soldiers alike out of bed. A month later they
repeated the process and brought in more. In all,
there were over 500 warrants issued. Though the
Grecos and Totò Riina remained underground, the
operation was a brilliant success. Three of the warrants were for the ex-land-assessor and Mayor of
Palermo, Vito Ciancimino, and the fabulously rich
cousins, Nino and Ignazio Salvo. The way to what
was known as 'the Third Level' of the Mafia had
been opened up.

Three months after the arrests of the Salvos—
again on the evidence of Buscetta and what the
American agencies had already found out via their
wiretaps and hidden microphones (including one

in a Mafia-boss's car)—the entire New York Commission was arrested: Paul 'Big Paulie' Castellano of the Gambino family, Phil 'Rusty' Rastelli of the Bonannos, Anthony 'Fat Tony' Salerno of the Genoveses, Tony 'Tony Ducks' Corallo of the Luccheses and Gennaro 'Gerry Lang' Langella, acting head of the Colombo family. Their average age was seventy years old. Their average bail was over $2 million each. They raised it in a matter of minutes.

After juridical moves, which involved some separate trials and the addition of other defendants, such as the by-now head of the Colombos, Carmine Persico, as well as one of the hit-men who'd killed Carmine Galante, Anthony 'Bruno' Indelicato, the trial opened on September 8, 1986. Buscetta was the first and most important witness for the prosecution. But there were others, including an assassin who had turned state's evidence because he couldn't bear to be separated from his boyfriend. There were also hours and hours of incriminating tapes. After listening to them all, the judge four months later sentenced all those accused of belonging to 'an ongoing criminal enterprise' to 100 years in prison each, except for Indelicato, who got forty-five for the murder of Galante. The judge said of one of the defendants, but it could have been applied to them all: 'You have essentially spent a lifetime terrorizing this community to your financial advantage.'

One defendant, though, was missing from the sentencing: Paul Castellano, who had been generally reckoned to be losing his grip, judging by the evidence of the tapes the American agencies—and now the defence lawyers—had been listening to. An edict against heroin he had issued several years previously had seriously destabilized his family. Now his own house had been bugged, he couldn't

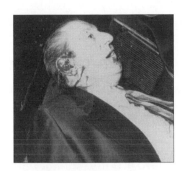

The corpse of 'Big Paulie', gunned down in Manhattan, December 1985

control the union-locals in his pocket, and he was intending to appoint as his underboss a man who was no more than a chauffeur but with whom he discussed Commission business. A few days before Christmas 1985, both he and the aspirant chauffeur were gunned down in front of Sparks Restaurant at Third Avenue and 46th Street in Manhattan by three men in trenchcoats and fedoras. The murder was almost certainly ordered by John Gotti, an ambitious *capo* in Castellano's Gambino family, but he must have had the say-so of the Commission.

The Maxi-Trial in Sicily

One month after the sentencing, in February 1986, what became called the 'maxi-trial' of the Sicilian Mafia began in a specially-built high-security bunker connected to the Ucciardone prison in Palermo. There were 456 defendants facing a wide variety of charges.

One of the Salvo cousins could not be present—he had died of cancer in a Swiss clinic; and Totò Riina was still underground. But Luciano Liggio was there, and so was Pippo Calò, the head of Buscetta's Porta Nuova family who'd become Cosa Nostra's emissary in Rome, where he had eleven apartments. In one of them, police had found eleven kilos of pure heroin, and in another a vast quantity of T4 explosive which was linked to a murderous 1984 bomb attack on a Naples-to-Milan express train—killing 16 and injuring 200—which until then was thought to have been the work of right-wing terrorists. The idea was to divert public attention from the testimony given by Buscetta and other informants. One late arrival was Michele 'The Pope' Greco, who was arrested after a dawn raid on a farmhouse twenty-five miles east of Palermo shortly after the trial began. Until then he had been tried *in absentia*.

The indictment—an extraordinary piece of work by Falcone and his team—ran to over 8000 pages and included the testimony now of a number of *pentiti*, among them a close ally and friend of Tommaso Buscetta. But it had been gathered together at a cost. In April 1985, a bomb attack had been made on an investigating magistrate in Trapani and though he'd escaped, a passing woman and her two children had been killed. Then in July and August 1986, within nine days of each other, the Palermo police chief, Giuseppe Montana, and the deputy head of his Flying Squad, Antonio Cassara, had been cut down. Half of Cassara's men had then successfully applied to be posted out of Sicily.

There were, however, signs of hope as the trial went on. Leoluca Orlando, a young radical politician, had been elected mayor of Palermo in July 1985, and he'd made the city an *ex parte* participant in the proceedings. He talked openly about the Mafia wherever he went and attended the maxi-trial, making a point of sitting with the families of Mafia victims. The city took heart and what became known as 'the Palermo Spring' was born. There were demonstrations of support from university students and local Jesuits mounted a campaign to persuade the Church, at last, to speak out against Cosa Nostra.

In the end the trial dragged on for almost two years. But 344 of the defendants were in the end found guilty. Nineteen life sentences were handed down to the bosses, among them Liggio, Pippo Calò and 'The Pope'. But the trial had failed to reach any higher than the foothills of what was called 'the Third Level' of the Mafia, the politicians who had backed and sustained it. It became clear that this network was still very active. During the investigation process, Falcone had told anyone who would listen that 'for months and months we've asked for men and means. . . but little has been done.' Now, after the trial, he was simply shunted aside. Another man was chosen to fill the post of the island's chief prosecutor—a man whose last case as a criminal prosecutor had been in northern Italy in 1949—and Falcone was forced to take up a job at the Ministry of Justice in Rome. Few new investigations were opened and there was a general fear that those convicted would soon have their sentences overturned in the appeals court—as had happened over and over again in the past. The flowers of 'the Palermo spring'—in the absence of any encouragement from the national government—began to wither away.

Just how far they'd withered away by 1991 became clear when a small Palermo businessman called Libero Grassi made public the fact that he was refusing to pay protection to the Mafia. He appeared on national television to denounce Mafia racketeering and was shortly thereafter casually shot down outside his house. For all 'the Palermo spring', virtually no-one outside his immediate family attended his funeral. It was the same old story, one that had effectively undermined so many trials in the past: no-one saw, no-one noticed, no-one could possibly say. However, fifteen years later, in October 2006, Mafiosi brothers Francesco and Salvino Madinia were convicted of Grassi's murder.

Giovanni Falcone Works Backstage

And yet something was happening behind the scenes: something that is even now very difficult to read. The prime minister between 1989 and 1992 had been Giulio Andreotti—and this period would in the end turn out to be crucial. Though Andreotti soon appointed as his Minister of the Interior a man who was later revealed to be a close associate of the Neapolitan Camorra, and though he campaigned vigorously for at least one blatantly Mafia candidate for parliament in Sicily, the fight against Cosa Nostra somehow went on. With Falcone's help inside the Ministry of Justice, new legislation was introduced, setting up a nationwide anti-Mafia police unit and an anti-Mafia prosecutor's office, among other things. Andreotti, in the meantime, under pressure, it is true, from both lawyers and public opinion in the aftermath of businessman Libero Grassi's death, refused to allow the release of those convicted in the maxi-trial pending their appeal.

There had already been one appeal in Palermo and the Mafia had won. The court had rejected what was called 'the Buscetta theorem', the idea that membership of the Commission during a particular period also meant responsibility for murders that had occurred during that period. But in summer 1991 was to come the big one: the final hearing of the case in the Supreme Court of Appeals in Rome, where it was generally expected that the sentences would be overturned. It was assumed that the case would come up before Judge Corrado Carnevale, who was known in legal circles as 'Amazzasentenze' or 'sentence-killer'. He'd already quashed the sentences of over 400 members of Cosa Nostra. According to later pentiti, the leaders of Cosa Nostra took it virtually for granted that their case would go the same way.

But it didn't. Under huge pressure from members of the parliament and the judiciary and from the Ministry of Justice, the president of the Court, who had the final word, appointed, instead of Carnevale, another judge with a reputation for complete honesty. In January 1992, the sentences were upheld.

Cosa Nostra Makes War on the State

Within two months after the decision to uphold the sentences, the Mafia declared war on the state. Their fixer in Rome, Salvo Lima, who was supposed to have made sure that things went Cosa Nostra's way, was gunned down by motor-cycle-riding assassins in the seaside resort of Mondello on March 12. Lima was thought to be an untouchable. He had been seven times mayor of Palermo and was a man of huge power, widely known, even in the European parliament in Strasbourg, as 'the viceroy of Sicily'. So his death—just as a new election campaign was beginning—was the clearest possible message to the centre: disobey us at your peril. Lima, as it happened, had been busily preparing for the arrival of Andreotti, due in a few days' time to support his Christian Democratic candidates. As it turned out, he had to come earlier, to attend Lima's funeral. He was, by all accounts, ashen: quite visibly shocked and shaken.

But Riina and the Commission didn't stop there. On May 23, Giovanni Falcone and his wife flew from Rome to spend the weekend at their house in Palermo. They were on a secret flight in a government plane and they were met at the airport by a cluster of bodyguards. But they also had another, secret, welcomer: a Mafia soldier who used a mobile phone to alert a group who were waiting above the airport and the turn-off of the airport road onto the freeway at Capaci. The group was keeping watch over a drainage channel under the freeway into which they'd stuffed 500 kilos of plastic explosive a few days before. As Falcone's motorcade approached, one of them pressed a detonator.

The bodyguards in the leading car were killed instantly, those in the car behind Falcone's only

Giovanni Falcone, the 'anti-Mafia' magistrate, pictured here with his wife. The Falcones were both killled by a Mafia bomb on May 23, 1992

slightly injured. But Falcone, who'd been driving the second car, and his wife, another magistrate, who'd been beside him, died that night, shortly after being taken to hospital.

Falcone's friend Paolo Borsellino, who'd taken over his old job in Palermo at the end of 1991, arrived in the emergency room in time to see him die. People said later that he seemed to make a pledge there. He began to work harder afterwards than he ever had: interviewing the new *pentiti* who'd appeared, following up and cross-referencing their stories. His assistant prosecutor said: 'He was a man in a tremendous hurry. . . someone who knew that his hours were numbered. . . He felt that time was running out on him.'

On July 19, just as news from Milan was further exposing just how widespread all over Italy corruption really was, time did run out. Borsellino, after taking a rare Sunday off, made a call to his mother in Palermo that he was coming to pay her a visit. The call, though, was picked up, and a primed car was hurriedly placed outside his mother's apartment building. When Borsellino arrived, his six bodyguards spread out, holding their machine guns at the ready. But then the car-bomb went off, and all seven, one of them a woman, were blown to pieces. The apartments facing the road were destroyed all the way up to the fourth floor, though the road where the car had been was thirty feet away.

Between the deaths of Falcone and Borsellino, Judge Carrado Carnevale of the Supreme Court of Appeals delivered himself of a judgment in another Mafia case arising out of the maxi-trial organized by Falcone. He'd said that there was no such thing as a Commission or a Cupola, no such person as a Don and no such people as 'Men of Honour', in effect parrotting the old Sicilian line of 'Mafia? Who?'.

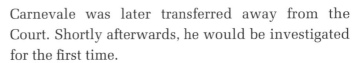

Carnevale was later transferred away from the Court. Shortly afterwards, he would be investigated for the first time.

In 1993, Carnevale was suspended due his ties with Giulio Andreotti who faced trial for his Mafia

Paolo Borsellino, a friend of Giovanni Falcone, was killed on July 19, 1992 by a car bomb outside his apartment in Capaci

links. In 2001, Carnevale was sentenced to six years in jail for criminal conspiracy with the Mafia. The verdict was reversed the following year and he was returned to the bench in 2007.

The Funerals: The Public Reacts

The deaths of Falcone and Borsellino, though, changed much. Some 40,000 people attended the first funeral of Falcone and the other victims of 'the massacre at Capaci'. At the service the distraught young widow of one of the policemen literally ordered the assembled leaders of the country to their knees. After remembering and praising her husband, she said: 'The state, the state: why are mafiosi still inside the state? I pardon you, but get down on your knees. But they don't change—too much blood. There's no love here, there's no love here, there's no love here. There's no love at all.'

Soon sheets inscribed with slogans appeared on balconies all over Palermo: 'Falcone, you continue to live in our hearts'; 'I know but I don't have the proof'; 'Palermo has understood, but has the state?' These soon spread to schools. There were demonstrations and work projects. Students even went to a village where there had recently been Mafia wars and symbolically took it over for a day.

After the second death, though, the mood changed to one of anger and despair. Borsellino's wife refused the offer of a state funeral. But when one was duly held in Palermo Cathedral for the bodyguards who'd been killed, the national politicians and the chief of Palermo's police had to be protected from the fury of the crowds and from that of many of the police officers present. The scandal of *Tangentopoli* ('Bribesville')—the elaborate system of bribes and kickbacks at every level of the Italian state—was beginning to reach government figures at the highest level and the future looked horribly bleak. *The Observer* of London wrote at the time: 'The country is in a state of chaos, a state of war. It has the highest murder rate in the European Community, the most rampant and blatant corruption, an ailing economy, a floundering government, and an anguished and embarrassed population.'

Totò Riina Arrested: The Emergence of the *Pentiti*—and of Giulio Andreotti

For the citizens of Palermo, however, there was a little hope. In the aftermath of Borsellino's death, 7,000 troops were sent to Sicily to boost their morale. Not long afterwards a senior Mafioso was captured, and so, finally, on January 15, 1993, was Totò Riina, after living 'underground' for twenty-four years. 'Who are you?' was the first question Riina asked as he was bundled out of a car and flung down onto a Palermo sidewalk. He seemed to have expected some sort of coup attempt from inside the Cosa Nostra—anyone but undercover police—and appeared relieved by the answer. The man who'd led the police commando to him was a recent *pentito* called Baldassare Di Maggio who believed that Riina had condemned him to death. Once arrested by the police, he'd realized he had finally run out of options. 'I'm a dead man,' he'd said, 'but I am a man of honour. I can take you to Riina.'

With Riina taken, a number of *pentiti* who'd earlier agreed to give evidence on the grounds, in the words of one of them, that 'Cosa Nostra has undertaken an irreversible strategy of death', began to sing a new song. In their safe houses all over Italy and, in Buscetta's case, somewhere in the United States, they began to sing about Andreotti. And it was their and their country's great good luck that the man who listened to them was a man called Gian Carlo Caselli, Palermo's recently-appointed new chief prosecutor and, in the words of historian Paul Ginsborg, 'quite the most courageous and dedicated public servant in the Europe of his time.' It was Caselli, after he'd heard them out, who in March 1993 formally informed Andreotti, the longest-serving politician of the Italian Republic and six times Prime Minister, that he was under investigation for collusion with Cosa Nostra.

Totò Riina in court

22

The Politics of the Mafia

ONE ENTERS THE WORLD of post-war Italian politics at one's peril. It was a maze of constantly shifting alliances and power blocs, of continually changing governments and of treacherous new conformations, of favours granted and called in and traded. And the whole thing, the whole murky midden of Byzantine manoeuvrings, was fuelled by a compost of patronage and money.

Put at its simplest, politicians in the post-war period had more resources at their disposal than at any other time in the history of Italy and they were able to channel these resources in more or less any direction they wished. It made the best possible sense, then, for them to use this financial clout of theirs to help them remain in office: i.e. to build up a power base via those who now owed them for having been favoured.

Since this was very much the way in which the Sicilian Mafia itself worked, it was relatively easy for them to insert themselves into this system of distribution which, to put it very crudely, meant money in return for votes. So they organized many of the local offices of the Christian Democrats, attracted new members and delivered the votes. When it became clear that this was what was necessary, they moved to take control of such local municipal governments that they didn't already own.

This was a crucial step, since controlling municipal government, particularly in Palermo, gave them the freedom to operate without any hindrance: to pollute and to jerrybuild and to get building licences whenever and wherever they wanted them. This was triumphantly achieved during the time of the great construction boom at the end of the Fifties, when two of their own, Salvo Lima and Vito Ciancimino, became mayor and overseer of public works respectively in the same Palermo administration. Buscetta later claimed that Lima's father was a 'made' Mafia man, and Ciancimino was almost certainly inducted into the Corleonese family that came to be controlled by Totò Riina. Both were, though, at the least in constant contact with the Mafia, as were their friends Nino and Ignazio Salvo, who made their first fortunes in the lucrative business of tax-collecting.

Once this first step had been achieved (obtaining the freedom to act locally without hindrance or even much interest from its patrons in Rome, just so long as the votes were delivered), the tentacles of *la piovra*, the Mafia octopus, began inevitably to reach upwards. Salvo Lima, by the time he became a national MP in 1968, was both immensely powerful and extremely rich—and he chose the man to whom he now offered the rich plum of Sicily very carefully indeed.

Salvo Lima, the Salvos and the 'Apotheosis'

Giulio Andreotti
always maintained
strong links with
Sicily

Giulio Andreotti—bat-eared, hunchbacked, bespectacled—had emerged after the War from the Vatican and various Catholic student organizations to become a minister in 1947, aged twenty-eight. He'd served in virtually every government thereafter, but he had never yet been prime minister, for his group and influence in the Christian Democrats was too narrowly based. With Lima's help in Sicily, he was

at last able to get what he wanted. And so too could Lima and his friends.

The *Andreottani*, as they became known in the island, soon achieved a reputation for unbridled corruption and though Andreotti himself always claimed to have no knowledge at all about what went on there, this notion flies in the face of his reputation as an endless and subtle collector of facts. He regularly visited the island for electoral campaigns and put time aside to discuss Sicilian matters. When the corrupt Ciancimino, having failed to build his own power-base in Sicily, came to visit him in November 1976 to make peace, he and Salvo Lima were graciously received in Andreotti's prime ministerial office. Lima described the meeting as 'aimed at establishing a general pacification of Palermo'.

In 1979, Andreotti flew to Palermo to address a huge rally on behalf of Salvo Lima's candidacy for the European Parliament. To the strains of the national anthem, he arrived on stage with Lima, to be surrounded there by all the major Sicilian players: Piersanti Mattarella, the regional president of the Christian Democrats (shot the following year), their secretary, Rosario Nicoletti (a suicide in 1984 after being accused of collusion with Cosa Nostra), Vito Ciancimino (arrested and convicted as a Mafioso five years later, the first Italian politician to be found guilty of Mafia membership), and Nino Salvo (arrested in the run-up to the maxi-trial but died before sentencing—cousin Ignazio was shot in Palermo in 1992 after being convicted). The rally was followed by a banquet for 300 in the Salvos' Hotel Zagarella outside Palermo. The whole occasion, said a later witness, was 'like an apotheosis'—though Andreotti later claimed not to have known the Salvos at all.

Andreotti Meets the Commission

In 1980, for all this, Andreotti was back in Palermo again, via a private plane hired by the Salvos, for his first direct meeting with the Commission. He was there to find out why Piersanto Mattarella had been killed, and the venue was a Mafia-owned hunting-lodge outside the city. Lima and the Salvos were also there and one of the later *pentiti*, who'd been on guard outside the house, heard shouting. Stefano Bontate, the Cosa Nostra boss who was in charge of relations with the politicians and was assassinated by Riina a year later, later told him the message that had been given to Andreotti: 'In Sicily we give the orders. And if you don't want to wipe out the [Christian Democrats] completely, you do what we say. Otherwise we'll take away your vote. Not only in Sicily but. . . all over southern Italy. You'll only be able to count on the vote up north, and up there they all vote communist anyway. You can make do with that.'

Buscetta, who was a close friend of Bontate's, later described Andreotti's Christian Democrats as 'the political faction of the Cosa Nostra'. Another Mafioso *pentito*, who'd been a Palermo councillor, went further. He called the Christian Democrats a virtual Mafia family, one in which Andreotti was known to the Sicilians as 'Uncle Giulio', in exactly the same way as Riina was known as 'Uncle Totò'. Andreotti, Lima and Bontate almost certainly had a further connection—through Masonry, common membership of a secret masonic lodge called Propaganda Due (P2)—and thereby hangs a very dark tale indeed.

23

The Scandal of P2: Roberto Calvi, The Vatican and the Mafia

I N MARCH 1981, a finance-police force, acting under the order of magistrates investigating Michele Sindona's bank collapse, raided a villa outside Florence owned by the financier Licio Gelli and found in his office a partial membership list of a hitherto secret lodge, P2. He was its Worshipful Master. The list, which started at the number 1600, included the names of all the heads of the secret services, twelve generals of the *carabinieri*, five of the Finance Police, twenty-two of the army, four of the air force and eight admirals. Fourteen judges were there, forty-four members of parliament and ten bank presidents. So were the names of Michele Sindona, of the dead journalist Mino Pecorelli and of a businessman and future prime minister called Silvio Berlusconi.

The police also found in Gelli's house files of top-secret material which Gelli must have received from the secret-service members of P2, and which were apparently intended to be used—or had

Ex-Socialist President
Bettino Craxi eventually
took up residence in Tunis
for twenty-five years

already been used—for black-mail purposes. There was clear evidence, too, of a P2 plot to instigate a right-wing takeover of government—and also a curious document, relating to the deposit of $7 million into the Swiss bank account of the secretary of the Socialist Party, Bettino Craxi, by banker and P2 member Roberto Calvi.

Masonry in Italy had been banned under Mussolini, but was reborn under American influence after the Second World War as a secret bastion against communism. By 1971, though, it was clear that it had done little to counter the social upheavals of the previous decade. So the Grand Master of one of the Masons' most powerful groupings, the Grande Oriente d'Italia, asked the unrepentant fascist Gelli to reconsitute an old lodge called 'Propaganda' as P2.

Documents later found in a briefcase being smuggled out of the country by Gelli's daughter made clear who P2's enemies were: the communist party and the trade-union movement. The aim, in the end, was 'overall control' of the government—to be achieved via a programme of extensive corruption. P2 had already bought Italy's leading newspaper, the *Corriere della Sera*, and its capital had been expanded with the help of an investment from the Vatican's own bank, the Institute of Religious Works, which was controlled by Chicago-born Archbishop Paul Marcinkus.

By the time the smuggled briefcase was found, Roberto Calvi—whose connections with the

Roberto Calvi
(inset) was found
hanging from
Blackfriars Bridge
in London

Vatican and Marcinkus had earned him the nick-name of 'God's Banker'—was dead, found hanged under Blackfriars Bridge in London. His bank, the Banco Ambrosiano, which had taken over the job of laundering the Mafia's drug money from Sindona, had recently collapsed with debts of $1.3 billion. The coroner's court in London pronounced his death a suicide but a further enquiry in 1993 agreed that he had been murdered, possibly by the Masons as P2 members referred to themselves as 'frati neri' or 'black friars'. By that time Italian *pentito* Francesco Marino Mannoia had named the man who killed him: a convicted Mafia drugs trafficker called Franco Di Carlo, acting on the orders of Licio Gelli and Pippo Calò. The briefcase Calvi had had with him in London had reappeared—if only briefly. It and its contents had been bought by a Vatican bishop for an eight-figure dollar sum and the cheques had been drawn on the Vatican bank controlled by Marcinkus.

Both Marcinkus and the bishop were exempt from prosecution in Italy as citizens of the sovereign state of the Vatican. Gelli was arrested in Switzerland and brought back, but made an escape from prison by helicopter and fled for his estates in Uruguay. And though he was subsequently extradited back to Italy, again from Switzerland, the terms of his extradition meant that he could only be tried on financial charges relating to the collapse of the Banco Ambrosiano, though he had been formally charged with the murder of Roberto Calvi. He was later convicted of being the paymaster for a bomb-attack in 1980 at Bologna Central Station which cost eighty-five lives—but he never served time. Only General Gianadelio Maletti of the secret services was ever given an unsuspended sentence in the matter of P2—and by that time he'd fled to South Africa. Bettino Craxi, the Socialist ex-Prime Minister, later went the same way, taking up residence in his house in Tunis, from where he couldn't be extradited, and sentenced to twenty-five years for corruption in his absence.

Franco Di Carlo turned *pentito*, but denied he had killed Roberto Calvi, though he had been asked to do so by Pippo Calò. Di Carlo said the killers were Sergio Vaccari and Vincenzo Casillo, who belonged to the Camorra in Naples and have since been killed. In July 2003, however, Pippo Calò, Flavio Carboni, Manuela Kleinszig, Ernesto Diotallevi, and Calvi's ex-driver and bodyguard Silvano Vittor went on trial for the murder in a specially fortified courtroom in Rome's Rebibia prison. In June 2007, all five were acquitted as there was 'insufficient proof' to convict them of murder. The acquittal was upheld by the Court of Cassation in November 2011.

The Mafia and the Masons

How far was the Mafia involved in P2? The answer is that no-one really knows. But some senior members of Cosa Nostra were certainly involved alongside Lima, Calvi and Sindona; there may very well have been a network of provincial lodges allied to it, particularly in Sicily and Calabria. A high officer of the Grand Orient Lodge has given evidence of links between masonry and the Mafia and another Grand Master even went so far as to examine the records of his own lodge, and then promptly resigned, saying 'I have seen a monster'. There is evidence, too, that in the late 1970s, Mafia members joined masonic lodges in significant numbers and Palermo Mayor Leoluca Orlando has always insisted that Cosa Nostra and masonry are now crucially interlinked.

Evidence of this interlinkage surfaced as the result of work done by a magistrate in Calabria who was investigating a European Economic Community (EEC) fraud. He uncovered letters between Gelli and a local Calabrian masonic lodge and was later able to name Gelli, along with 128 others, as deeply implicated in an arms-, drugs- and precious metals-trafficking network he had uncovered. The investigation, though, got no further. The magistrate's staff was immediately cut in half and promotion denied him. He later claimed that corrupt police officers in criminal-dominated lodges were impeding his work and provided the Council of the Judiciary with a list of magistrate-masons who were helping organized crime. He even told the

anti-Mafia commission in Rome that one of its own members was a hitherto-unknown member of P2.

In the end, the whole P2 affair more or less disappeared, even though the first news of it had brought down the government of the day. The judicial inquiry was taken out of the hands of the magistrates and transferred to the prosecutor's office in Rome, where a judge in 1994 ultimately pronounced that P2 was a 'normal' Masonic lodge, and secret only to 'the deaf and illiterate'. The Supreme Court's judgment was more balanced, but it basically agreed that P2 was not a conspiracy but 'a business committee'!

And was the Grand Master of this 'business committee' really Giulio Andreotti—as Roberto Calvi's widow swore he was? Most Italians couldn't believe that he wasn't, since the master manipulator seemed to have a finger in every pie. But there has never been any evidence one way or the other. Andreotti did agree that he'd once bumped into Gelli at the official Buenos Aires residence of the Argentinian dictator Juan Peròn, but had only known him before that as the head of a company making mattresses. He said on a chat show: 'I thought, "There's someone who looks just like the managing director of the Permaflex mattress factory in Frosinone".'

The Kiss: The Summit between Andreotti and Riina

Argentinian
dictator Juan Peròn

Andreotti did, though, know Totò Riina—or so said the *pentito* Baldassare Di Maggio who'd been Riina's driver and had fingered him to the Palermo police. In 1993, once Riina was safely behind bars, Di Maggio spoke to investigators of a day during the Chistian Democrats' annual Friendship Festival in September 1987, when he'd been asked to pick up 'Uncle Totò' for an important meeting.

Andreotti had been in Palermo that day, to stay at the Villa Igiea hotel and to give two talks: the first in the morning and the second at six o' clock in the evening. He had some time off, so he dismissed his guards and agreed to rendezvous with them later in the day. He didn't take lunch with the others in the hotel restaurant. He, in effect, disappeared.

Baldassare di Maggio, meanwhile, went to pick up Totò Riina, as agreed, and took him to the house where Ignazio Salvo, under house arrest while awaiting sentence from the maxi-trial, was living. Di Maggio later described the layout of the house in great detail, as well as the furnishings of the sitting-room suite into which the two men were led by Salvo's Mafia driver/assistant. Three men were sitting there, he said: Ignazio Salvo, Salvo Lima and Giulio Andreotti, 'whom I recognized without a shadow of a doubt.' Di Maggio added that he kissed Ignazio Salvo and shook hands with the others before retiring to another room, but 'Riina, on the other hand, kissed all three persons, Andreotti, Lima and Salvo.'

In the Mafia, a kiss sometime signifies a sentence of death. But it is also the ultimate sign of respect. It symbolized on this occasion that it was a meeting between equals, a summit meeting between heads of state. 'Uncle Totò' and 'Uncle Giulio' were meeting to discuss matters of life importance—and perhaps of death too.

Whatever was said, the meeting, Di Maggio claimed, lasted three or three and a half hours. He took it for granted that its subject was the maxi-trial, which had been going on for a year and a half by then and still had another three months to run. The Cosa Nostra had tried everything to wreck it. They'd tried to have the judge removed for bias and misconduct—and had failed. They'd also demanded that all the documents in the case—over 8000 pages of them—should be read aloud in court, so that the trial would carry on over the time legally allowed for defendants to remain in custody—but the Italian parliament had passed a new law specifically to prevent this. What Riina must have wanted to know was why on earth the Christian Democrats hadn't done more to stop this new law. He must also have demanded some guarantees from Andreotti for the future.

Riina, after the meeting, kept quiet. Di Maggio simply drove him back home. As for Andreotti, he reappeared at his hotel, met up with his body-guards, and arrived just in time for his second talk of the day.

Andreotti on Trial

Andreotti was brought to trial twice during the 1990s

By the time this partial eyewitness account became public knowledge, Andreotti had been passed over for President of the Republic because of the clouds gathering about his name. Instead, he'd been made Senator for Life as a sort of consolation prize. But this meant that he had lifelong immunity from prosecution, an immunity which now had to be removed if he was ever to be tried. By this time, however, Buscetta had given testimony to the senate, claiming that Andreotti headed in effect the political wing of the Mafia, and another of the *pentiti* had said bluntly: 'The most powerful political reference point for Cosa Nostra was Senator Andreotti.' The Palermo magistrates also brought in as evidence a private diary that had been kept by the murdered General Dalla Chiesa. In this diary—of which the magistrates said: 'It can be ruled out that the general would have written falsehoods in a completely personal document'—Dalla Chiesa had

John Paul II found time in the
Vatican to clasp Andreotti's
hands fervently between his
own in a photo opportunity
the media described as 'almost
an embrace'

recorded a number of meetings with Andreotti, then the Prime Minister. In one meeting he had complained of not getting enough backing from the Christian Democrats—and Andreotti had replied obliquely. He'd told the story of Pietro Inzerillo, whose dead body had been shipped back to Sicily with dollars stuffed into his mouth. Andreotti was definitely implying, said the magistrates, that the General should think before he went too far.

At another meeting, Dalla Chiesa told Andreotti that he was not going to favour any Christian Democratic politicians who might be involved in corruption. Andreotti was recorded as having 'gone white' at this news.

With his immunity lifted, Andreotti was first questioned in December 1993. He had, of course, a completely different memory of his meetings with Dalla Chiesa. He also said he had never known either of the Salvos (both of whom were by now dead, as was Salvo Lima). Even when confronted with Baldassare Di Maggio, he remained completely calm.

Nevertheless he came to trial in Palermo in 1995 for association and collusion with Cosa Nostra and was further arraigned in Perugia for the murder of Mino Pecorelli. Between the staggered starts of the two trials, in the words of author Peter Robb in his brilliant *Midnight in Sicily*: 'His Holiness Pope John Paul II found time in the Vatican to clasp Andreotti's hands fervently between his own in a photo opportunity the media described as "almost an embrace". The former prime minister seemed heartened by the Holy Father's attention; but a student challenged the Pope from the pulpit of St. Peter's over this; and it was the first time a pope had been challenged in his own church in seven hundred years.'

24

A Change of Allegiance: The Rise of Silvio Berlusconi and Forza Italia

B Y NOW, the political dispensations which had ruled Italy since the War had more or less completely disintegrated because of the welter of charges brought against politicians and bureaucrats all over the country in what became known as *Tangentopoli*. Besides, with the Berlin Wall down and the threat from Russia neutered, America felt much less inclined to prop up an administration which, with its help and encouragement, had become terminally corrupt.

The Cosa Nostra agreed. In the 1994 elections, ex-P2-member Silvio Berlusconi and his recently-founded party Forza Italia swept to power in Italy—and notably, too, in Sicily. It was said that the new Cosa Nostra boss on the ground, Giovanni Brusca, had decided to punish the Christian Democrats where it most hurt. Brusca was the man who'd thrown the detonator switch which had blown up Giovanni Falcone. He'd also had the twelve-year-old son of one of the *pentiti* held for two years, then finally strangled and dissolved in acid. The murder was said to have been carried out on his behalf by Totò Riina's teenage son—he was later charged for it—who bowed to the body, according to the ancient custom, before it was thrown into the vat. Though Forza Italia lost the next national election in 1996, it still held on to Sicily—thanks in part to Giovanni Brusca, who had made it his business in the interim to kill as many of the *pentiti's* relatives as he could find.

The Mafia Picks up the Pieces

Psychopathic Giovanni Brusca was arrested in 1996

There were some successes as the Andreotti trial dragged on. Brusca was finally picked up in 1996, and not long afterwards, another important lieutenant of Riina's, Leoluca Bagarella. Gian Carlo Caselli also successfully prosecuted Bruno Contrada, who'd been head of the investigative police force in Palermo before rising to third in command of the Italian secret services. It was Contrada, said the *pentiti*—who by now numbered over 500—who had been responsible for Totò Riina's 23-year-long avoidance of capture.

The trial of Giulio Andreotti on Mafia charges in Palermo dragged on for over three years, ending in 1999 with his acquittal. However, in 2002 he was sentenced to twenty-four years in jail for the murder of the journalist Mino Pecorelli, who had published allegations that Andreotti had ties to the Mafia. But the 83-year-old Andreotti was immediately released pending appeal and in 2003 his conviction was overturned by Italy's highest court. Prime Minister Silvio Berlusconi condemned the acquittal and the judge in Perugia that had originally found him guilty was given police protection after receiving a death threat. Palermo justice remained unreliable, to say the very least. One Mafia boss, Vito Vitale—who'd been captured to enormous fanfare—was also released without having to go through the charade of an appeal; and Totò Riina was actually found innocent, for the first time in his life, of the murder of a judge—though he remained in jail convicted of over a hundred murders.

It was a measure of the continuing power of Cosa Nostra that in 1998 a high-level meeting of the Sicilian *capi* was actually held behind the walls of Ucciardone prison, with guests from outside staying overnight before being sent on their way. This event, widely reported in Sicilian newspapers, was described as consisting of 'constructive discussions'. Giovanni Brusca, behind bars for the kidnapping and strangulation of the *pentito*'s young son, was said to have made a moving speech about the importance of human values. He was, in the words of Norman Lewis in his book *In Sicily*, 'assured by those present that this was the common aim'.

Bernardo 'The Tractor' Provenzano

Finally arrested in 2006: Provenzano

Perhaps, in a sense, it now is. Certainly the yearly murder rate in Sicily has dropped from several hundreds to double figures. With Brusca behind bars, the only major known Mafia figure still at large was Riina's lieutenant Bernardo Provenzano, who turned against the bombing campaign that had brought the Mafia such bad publicity. He also tried to stem the flow of *pentiti*, not by targeting their families, but by trying to re-establish the old Mafia rules undermined by Riina and Liggio, and using violence only when absolutely necessary. He communicated only by courier via typewritten notes—'*pizzini*'—which characteristically started: 'Dearest, in the hope that this finds you in the best of health' and ended: 'May the Lord bless and protect you.' Although Provenzano was known in his youth as *U Tratturi*—'The Tractor'—because, as one *pentiti* put it, 'he mows people down', he later became known as 'The Accountant' for his gentler style of leadership and his systematic infiltration of public finances.

In 2006, Provenzano, then seventy-three, was arrested in a small farmhouse outside his home town of Corleone, after police had followed fresh laundry sent by his wife. He had been on the run for forty-three years.

He had been convicted in absentia of more than twelve murders, including those of Giovanni Falcone and Paolo Borsellino. Ten more arrest warrants were outstanding. Fifty-seven other Mafiosi were jailed for a total of 300 years for protecting him while he was in hiding.

Provenzano's first court appearance was by video link from the high-security jail in Terni, central Italy. He appeared on screen alongside Totò Riina, another inmate, who Giovanni Brusca claims had been 'sold' to the Carabinieri by Provenzano in exchange for an archive of compromising material that Riina held.

Both men were handed multiple life sentences, which they are currently serving in solitary confinement, communicating only with their lawyers. Though they both appealed for release on health grounds in 2011, it is unlikely they will ever taste freedom again.

25

The Godfather and The Goodfellas: the Mafia Grows Old and Rich– but Lives On

The Mafia is not what it was. In America it became something of a laughing stock. After the murder of Paul Castellano, John Gotti took over the Gambino family. Instead of keeping a low profile, Gotti appeared in public wearing $10,000 hand-made suits and quickly became known as 'The Dapper Don'. In his neighbourhood in Queens, he organized lavish street parties and festivals, and was praised by local people for keeping crime out of the area. In Little Italy, he would shake hands and pose for pictures with tourists outside the Ravenite Social Club, where he conducted business, and he basked in the media spotlight.

Gotti had served time in both state and federal prison, and had even been jailed for manslaughter. He had shot an Irish-American gangster named James McBratney in front of witnesses in a tavern on Staten Island in 1973, after McBratney had kidnapped and murdered Carlo Gambino's son. Nevertheless, as head of the Gambino family, Gotti quickly became known to the media as the 'Teflon Don' when he beat two seemingly watertight cases for racketeering and assault by bribing or threatening jurors. Nothing seemed to stick.

With informants inside the police department, Gotti kept one step ahead of the NYPD. However, he had come to the attention of the FBI, who bugged his phones, his club and other places of business. To get around this, he used public phones, held meetings walking down the street and played loud tapes of white noise. But eventually the FBI taped him in an apartment above the club discussing a number of murders and other criminal activities—and, crucially, they caught Gotti on tape denigrating his underboss Salvatore 'Sammy The Bull' Gravano. On 11 December 1990, FBI agents and New York City detectives raided the Ravenite Social Club and arrested Gotti, Gravano, Frank Locascio and Thomas Gambino. Gotti was charged with loansharking, racketeering, obstruction of justice, illegal gambling, tax evasion, conspiracy and thirteen counts of murder. Among the alleged victims were Paul Castellano and Thomas Bilotti, Castellano's driver.

The case against Gotti was overwhelming. Not only did the FBI have Gotti on tape, they had several witnesses. Philip Leonetti, former underboss of the Philadelphia crime family, testified that Gotti had bragged that he had ordered the hit on Castellano. Armed with the tapes, federal prosecutors persuaded 'Sammy The Bull' Gravano, who was with Gotti when Castellano was killed, to testify against his boss on the promise of a reduced sentence and safekeeping under the Witness

Reputed mob boss
John Gotti arrives at
court in New York
on assault and
conspiracy charges,
1990

Protection Program. The trial became a media circus, with movie actor Mickey Rourke and other celebrities jostling for seats.

On 2 April 1992, Gotti was found guilty on all charges and sentenced to 100 years in prison. He was sent to the United States Penitentiary at Marion, Illinois, where he was kept in an underground cell, measuring just eight foot by seven (about 2.5x2 m), for 23 hours a day with only a radio and a small black-and-white TV set for company. His meals were shoved through a slot in the door and he was allowed two showers a week. The one-hour a day he was allowed out of the cell, he spent alone in an exercise yard surrounded by a concrete wall. To all intents and purposes, he was held in solitary confinement, but at least the federal authorities could be sure that he was not continuing to run the family business from jail.

Gotti died of throat cancer in jail on 10 June 2002. The Roman Catholic Diocese of Brooklyn refused a mass for his burial. By then the Gambino family had been taken over by his son John Gotti Jr, who pleaded guilty to racketeering, bribery, extortion and threatening violence in 1999. More charges followed. However, he claimed to have given up his life of crime, though he refused to testify against others.

While the Gottis attracted the media attention, other New York crime families could go about their business in the shadows. Meantime, the media gave the Mafia a make-over. *The Godfather* movies, based on the 1969 book by Mario Puzo, made

Marlon Brando in
Francis Coppola's
The Godfather: an
example of how the
Mafia are perceived
and have been
popularized in
modern culture

people nostalgic for a time when 'men of honour' put their family first. Black humour was added to the mix in *Goodfellas* and, in 1999, the Mafia entered the living room with the long-running series *The Sopranos*.

Things were also changing in Sicily. With Bernardo Provenzano in jail, Mafiosi began a power struggle over who would be the next *capo di tutti i capi*—'boss of all bosses'.

'We should not make the mistake of thinking that the arrest of Bernardo Provenzano will mean the beginning of the end of the Mafia,' said Sicily's leading anti-Mafia magistrate Antonio Ingroia. 'There is a generation of fifty-somethings ready to carry on.'

He named at least two people qualified to take Provenzano's place: Salvatore Lo Piccolo and Matteo Messina Denaro. A gang boss from the Resuttana district of Palermo, 63-year-old Lo Piccolo was the closest to Provenzano and considered 'old school'. Denaro was just 46. From the impoverished western Sicilian provincial city of Castelvetrano, he was known as the 'playboy boss' because of his passion for gold watches, fast cars and beautiful women. Like Riina and Provenzano, both men had been on the run for some time—Lo Piccolo since 1983, Denaro since 1993. Other key players in the power struggle were Totò Riina's physician Antonio Cinà, builder Francesco Bonura, pioneer of the heroin refineries Gerlando Alberti and Nino Rotolo, a henchman of Luciano Liggio and convicted gangster who was kept under house arrest due to a medical condition.

When it was clear that the 'Pax Mafiosa'—which had held since Provenzano took over in 1993—was falling apart, the police swooped on fifty-two bosses and forty-five 'capimandamento' (district bosses) and acting bosses—among them Cinà, Bonura, Alberti and Rotolo, though seven suspects avoided capture. The code Provenzano used in his pizzini had been broken, providing the evidence needed for the arrests. Piles of these notes to his lieutenants were found in the farmhouse where Provenzano was captured.

Further evidence came from a bug in the Palermo flat that Francesco Bonura used as an office, and from the surveillance of a builders' hut next to the swimming pool of Nino Rotolo's villa, on the outskirts of the city. The police had secretly videoed the supposedly sick man vault the fence between the villa and the pool. It seems that Rotolo's doctor had given him pills to raise his blood pressure enough to get him out of jail.

In the steel-lined cabin, there were no phones or electronic equipment, just a table, eight plastic chairs and anti-bugging devices which Rotolo thought would make it impossible for police to listen in. He was wrong. Unaware that his security had been breached, Rotolo regularly hosted meetings with other mobsters in the hut with a football being placed outside the door as a signal to the sentries that a confidential session had begun.

From the evidence gathered, it became clear to the police that Rotolo—number 25 in Provenzano's numbered code—was planning a coup, along with his lieutenants Cinà and Bonura. Even while Provenzano was at large, Rotolo had assumed the authority to pass death sentences on other Mafia bosses. Transcripts of conversations in the cabin show him inveighing against a jailed clan chief, describing him as a 'pederast' because of a relationship he had had with an under-age girl.

'Even if he comes out aged 100, one of my lads will be there waiting for him,' Rotolo was recorded saying.

More crucially, it seems that Rotolo had passed a death sentence on Lo Piccolo and his son, Sandro. In September 2005, Rotolo was heard saying he was looking for barrels of sulphuric acid to dispose of their bodies. The two families had clashed over the remnants of the Inzerillo family, who had been exiled in the US since the Mafia war of the 1980s, where they had become involved with the Gambinos. Now they wanted to return to Sicily. Lo Piccolo was for their return, Rotolo against it.

'If they start shooting, I'll be the first to get it and then it will be your turn,' he told Bonura.

Killing the Lo Piccolos would have propelled Sicily into another Mafia war. Swift action on the part of the police and prosecutors had prevented it. However, it also revealed that the Mafia's political influence was undiminished. On 11 July 2006, Giovanni Mercadante, the regional deputy for Forza Italia, was arrested on suspicion of having Mafia connections. A hospital physician, he was thought to have been Bernardo Provenzano's doctor, while he was in hiding, in return for electoral favours.

He was found guilty and sentenced to 10 years and eight months in 2009, but released in February 2011 by the Palermo Court of Appeal.

It seems the battle is far from over. It also seems that life is not too hard on ex-Mafiosi. In Fortezza Medicea jail near Pisa, convicted mobsters have been allowed to open a restaurant, where a clientele vetted by the Ministry of Justice are served by multiple murderers. It has proved so popular that Italy's prison department are thinking of opening restaurants in other jails. Mafiosi, like other Italians it seems, take their food very seriously.

John Gotti visits his son's grave, March 1987

Index

Picture Credits

Images © Hulton Picture Library

Arcturus Publishing Limited has made every reasonable effort to
ensure that all permissions information has been sought and achieved
as required. However there may be inadvertent and occasional errors in
seeking permission to reproduce individual photographs for which
Arcturus Publishing Limited apologizes.